The Image of Black Women in Twentieth-Century South American Poetry:
A Bilingual Anthology

The Image of Black Women in Twentieth-Century South American Poetry:
A Bilingual Anthology

Edited and Translated by Ann Venture Young

An Original by Three Continents Press

© Ann Venture Young, 1987
Translations © Ann Venture Young, 1987

Three Continents Press
1636 Connecticut Avenue N.W.
Washington, D.C. 20009

All rights reserved. No part of this book may be reproduced in any manner whatsoever without written permission of the publisher, except for brief quotations in reviews and articles.

ISBN: 0-89410-275-3 (cloth)
       0-89410-276-1 (paper)
LC No.: 81-51644

Cover Art © Cheryl W. Hudson, 1987

For

Anna Scott Watson Venture
Clement Ira Venture ("Black Man")
Russell McKensey Young, Jr.
Russell Venture Young

Table of Contents

Preface/1

Introduction
   I. *Negras, Morenas,* and *Mulatas* in Peninsular Spanish Literature: From Hispano-Arabic Poetry to the Poetry of the Baroque/3

   II. *Negras, Morenas,* and *Mulatas* in New World Spanish Literature: From the Poetry of the Colonial Period to the Twentieth Century/13

   III. *Negras, Morenas,* and *Mulatas* in the Contemporary Poetry of Uruguay, Peru, Ecuador, Venezuela, and Colombia/29

Colombia/41

   Candelario Obeso/42
       La oberiencia filiá/44
       (Filial Obedience)
       Canción del boga ausente/48
       (Song of the Lonely Oarsman)

   Arturo Camacho Ramírez/51
       Bamba/52

   Hugo Salazar Valdés/56
       La negra María Teresa/58
       (The Black Girl María Teresa)
       Historia de Mary Bann/62
       (The Story of Mary Bann)
       Baile negro/66
       (Black Dance)

Helcías Martán Góngora/71
- Hada Madrina/72
  (Fairy Godmother)
- Preludio para Leonor González Mina/74
  (Prelude for Leonor Gonzalez Mina)
- Pejca/76
  (Fishin')
- Blasón/80
  (Family Emblem)
- Decir/82
  (A Saying)

Juan Zapata Olivella/85
- Negrita Claridad/86
  (The Black Girl Claridad)
- La mulata/90
  (Mulatto Woman)

Jorge Artel/95
- Bullerengue/96
  (Bullerengue)
- Danza, Mulata/98
  (**Dance, Mulatto**)
- La cumbia/100
  (The Cumbia)

Ecuador/103

Adalberto Ortiz/104
- Antojo/106
  (Caprice)
- Mosongo y la niña negra/110
  (Mosongo and the Black Girl)
- La tunda para el negrito/112
  (Bogey Man for a Little Black Boy)
- **Sábado y domingo/114**
  (Saturday and Sunday)
- Jolgorio/118
  (Frolic)

¿Qué tendrá la Soledad?/122
(What's the Matter with Soledad?)

Nelson Estupiñán Bass/125
    Negra bullanguera/126
    (Wild Black Girl)
    Tú sabías/128
    (You Knew)

Peru/131

Nicomedes Santa Cruz/133
    No es delito enamorar/134
    (It'sNot a Crime to Fall in Love)
    Ritmos negros del Perú/138
    (Black Rhythms of Peru)
    Cómo has cambiado, Pelona/142
    (My How You've Changed, Baldy)
    Que mi sangre se sancoche/146
    (Let My Blood Run Hot)
    Día de la madre/150
    (Mother's Day)

Uruguay/155

Virginia Brindis de Salas/156
    ¡Aleluya!/158
    (Hallelujah!)
    Semblanza/162
    (Portrait)
    Madrigal/164
    (Madrigal)
    La conga/166
    (The "Conga")
    Unguet/174
    (Unguet)
    Pregón número uno/178
    (*Pregón* Number One)
    Pregón número dos/182
    (*Pregón* Number Two)

Gastón Figueira/189
> Quitandeira/190
> (Candy Vendor)

Pilar E. Barrios/192
> Poema de la madre/194
> (The Mother's Poem)
>
> Negra/196
> (Black Woman)

Venezuela/203

Andrés Eloy Blanco/204
> Píntame angelitos negros/206
> (Paint Me Some Little Black Angels)

Manuel Rodríguez-Cárdenas/213
> Apunte para un "close-up" de Eusebia Cosme/214
> (Notes on a Close-Up of Eusebia Cosme)
>
> Canción de la negra Juana/216
> (Song of the "Negra" Juana)
>
> El merengue final/228
> (The Last Merengue)
>
> Tu risa/232
> (Your Smile)
>
> La canción de la negrita/234
> (The Song of the "Negrita")

Miguel Otero Silva/236
> La infancia/238
> (Childhood)

Works Cited/245
Works Consulted/248

Acknowledgments

I thank Helcías Martán Góngora for permission to reprint five poems from his *Suma Poética: 1963-1968* (Bogota: Biblioteca del Instituto Colombiano de Cultura Hispánica, 1969): "Hada Madrina," "Preludio para Leonor González Mina," "Pejca," "Blasón," and "Decir." The poems from Candelario Obeso: "La Oberiencia Filiá" and "Canción de la Boga Ausente" are from his *Cantos Populares de Mi Tierra* (Bogota: Biblioteca Popular de Cultura Colombiana, 1950). Arturo Camacho Ramírez's poem "Bamba" is from Rosa E. Valdés-Cruz, *La Poesía Negroide en América* (New York: Las Américas, 1970). The poems of Hugo Salazar Valdéz: "La Negra María Teresa" and "Baile Negro" are from his *Toda La Voz* (Bogota: Imprenta Nacional, 1958) and "Historia de Mary Bann" is from his *Las Raíces Sonoras* (Cali, 1976). The two poems from Juan Zapata Olivella: "Negrita Claridad" and "La Mulata" are from his *Albedrío Total* (Guatemala: José de Pineda Ibarra, 1970). Jorge Artel's "Bullerengue," "Danza, Mulata," and "La Cumbia" are from his *Tambores en la Noche* (Bogota: Ediciones Bolívar, 1940).

I also thank Nicomedes Santa Cruz for permission to reprint these poems and my translations of them: "Ritmos Negros del Perú," "Como Has Cambiado, Pelona," "Que Mi Sangre Se Sancoche," and "Día de la Madre" from his *Ritmos Negros del Perú* (Buenos Aires: Losada, 1971) and "No Es Delito Enamorar" in his *Décimas y Poemas: Antología* (Lima: Campodónico, 1971).

My thanks to Adalberto Ortiz for permission to reprint six of his poems and my translations of them: "Antojo," "Mosongo y la Niña Negra," "La Tunda para el Negrito"; "Sábado y Domingo" and "Jolgorio" from his *Tierra, Son y Tambor* (Mexico: La Cigarra, 1945), and "¿Qué Tendrá la Soledad?" from his *El Animal Herido* in his *Antología Poética* (Quito: Casa de la Cultura Ecuatoriana, 1959). I also thank Nelson Estupiñán Bass for permission to include two poems: "Negra Bullanguera" and "Tú Sabías" from his *Canto Negro por la Luz: Poemas para Negros y Blancos* (Esmeraldas: Ediciones del Núcleo Provincial de Esmeraldas de la Casa de la Cultura Ecuatoriana, 1954), and my translations.

I am grateful to Kraus Reprint for permission to reprint two poems by Pilar E. Barrios: "Poema de la Madre" and "Negra" which appear in the reprint of *Piel Negra: Poesías (1917-1947)* by Barrios. I likewise appreciate permission by Kraus Reprint to reprint a poem by Gastón Figueira: "Quitandeira," which appears in Emilio Ballagas, *Mapa de la Poesía Negra Americana* (Liechtenstein: Kraus Reprint, 1970). The poems by Virginia Brindis de Salas: "¡Aleluya!," "Unguet," "Semblanza," "Madrigal," "La

Conga," "Pregón Número Uno," and "Pregón Número Dos" are from her *Pregón de Marimorena* (Montevideo: Sociedad Cultural Editora Indoamericana, 1946).

My thanks to Manuel Rodríguez Cárdenas for permission to include five of his poems: "Apunte para un 'Close-Up' de Eusebia Cosme," "Canción de la Negra Juana," 'El Merengue Final,' "Tu Risa," and "La Canción de la Negrita" from his *Tambor: Poemas para Negros y Mulatos* (Caracas: Editorial "Elite," 1938). "Píntame Angelitos Negros" by Andrés Eloy Blanco is taken from Emilio Ballagas, *Mapa de la Poesía Negra Americana.* Miguel Otero Silva's "La Infancia" is from his *Poesía Completa* (Caracas: Monte Avila Editores, 1972).

Preface

Some of the earliest critical efforts in the field of Afro-Hispanic literature date back to the thirties. Subsequent critical studies by American and Latin American researchers and scholars continued to respond to the need to discover and interpret the significance of black writers and black fictional and poetic characters, but it was not until the late sixties and especially the seventies that the field of Afro-Hispanic literature began to receive appropriate levels of scholarly attention. The past decade alone produced major works of literary criticism by Lemuel Johnson, Miriam DeCosta, Mónica Mansour, and Richard L. Jackson. Works of this period are represented in anthologies covering Afro-Hispanic poetry and short stories by Rosa Valdés-Cruz, Stanley A. Cyrus, Jorge Luis Morales, Enrique Noble, and Hortensia Ruiz del Vizo.

However, despite this concerted and dedicated effort to interpret the presence and meaning of the black experience in Latin America, as expressed in the literature of these countries, little critical notice has been taken of the black woman, whose presence is central to Latin American literature and life. The chapter entitled "The Coloured Woman in Caribbean Literature" in G.R. Coulthard's *Race and Colour in Caribbean Literature*, my own essay, "Black Women in Afro-Caribbean Poetry," in DeCosta's *Blacks in Hispanic Literature*, Hector Pedro Blomberg's 1945 essay, "La negra y la mulata en la poesia americana," recent articles by Otto Olivera, Kay Boulware, and Stephanie Davis-Lett, and unpublished papers by Richard L. Jackson, Ken Lewis, and A. Faulkner Watts prevent the study of black women in Latin American literature from being a completely unexplored field.

The Image of Black Women in Twentieth-Century South American Poetry provides, probably for the first time, a representative selection of South American poetry in which the black female is the central figure. My translations make available to the English-speaking reader a body of literature which would otherwise be largely inaccessible. Further, this anthology could serve as a basis for subsequent studies of women in other literatures.

In selecting poems for inclusion in this collection, I was guided by the principles of artistic validity and thematic relevance. I have not attempted to heap critical praise on poetry that, although reflecting a "positive" visage of black women, has little artistic value. However, as suggested by Philip Butcher in his preface to *The Minority Presence in American Literature*, "I consider that an author's response to the minority presence of his time and place is part of his record as a person and an artist and should not be disregarded."

Given the epochal, geographic, and artistic diversity of the poets included in this anthology, a univocal image of the black woman could not be expected to emerge; rather, the various political, social, economic, and artistic circumstances yield a rich and varied imagery amenable to comparisons and contrasts on various critical levels.

The Image of Black Women in Twentieth-Century South American Poetry contains three introductory essays which provide an historical overview of the black woman, beginning with her appearance in Hispano-Arabic poetry and tracing her image through the poetry of the Spanish Baroque. The discussion continues, in the second essay, with an examination of the black woman in the poetry of the colonial New World through its expression in both the lyric and folk poetry of South America and the Caribbean. The final essay, "*Negras, Morenas,* and *Mulatas* in the Contemporary Poetry of Uruguay, Peru, Ecuador, Venezuela, and Colombia," examines the image of the black woman in the twentieth-century poetry of five South American countries.

This anthology includes the works of fifteen South American poets, all but one of whom were writing in the twentieth century. The lone exception is the Afro-Colombian poet, Candelario Obeso, who appears by virtue of his importance as a nineteenth-century precursor of black poetry in the Americas. All but two are of African descent, and one is a woman, Virginia Brindis de Salas of Uruguay. These poets are represented by 46 poems; biographical sketches precede each author's works.

I gratefully acknowledge the encouragement, support, and editorial assistance so generously given by Andress Taylor, Antonio G. Rodriguez, Ben C. Coleman, Stanley Cyrus, Eileen Crawford and Harriett Faulkner; my husband, Russell McKensey Young, Jr.; and my son, Russell Venture Young. A special note of appreciation must be extended to my former student, Marvin A. Lewis of the Romance Languages Faculty of the University of Illinois, Champaign-Urbana, for his tireless efforts in the discovery of many of the poems which were essential for this anthology.

I owe my inspiration to my mother, Anna Scott Watson Venture and my father, Clement Ira Venture ("Black Man") who prodded, cajoled, insulted, flattered, and loved me into trying to be the best Black woman I could be.

Introduction

I. *Negras, Morenas,* and *Mulatas* in Peninsular Spanish Literature: From Hispano-Arabic Poetry to the Poetry of the Baroque

The presence of blacks in Spain and Portugal between the 8th and the 13th centuries is well-documented. Most sub-Saharan Africans who arrived during this period of Muslim rule were slaves. There was a clear preference for the importation of African female slaves to serve primarily as domestic workers and concubines, while male slaves often served in the military.[1] The status of all African slaves, of course, varied considerably from one period of the Muslim era to another. Some periods favored the possibility of manumission while others were less propitious.

Spanish Christian merchants entered the slave trade as early as the 11th century and continued to import slaves into Spain until at least the 15th century.[2] The Portuguese slave traders, who began on a small scale in the 13th century, continued to supply Spain with slave labor for several centuries.

The early presence of blacks in the Iberian Peninsula is evidenced in Hispano-Arabic literature, principally in lyric poetry written in Mozarabic, which dates back to the 10th century.[3] The female figure dominates much of this poetry, in which white was synonymous with feminine beauty. However, when an African was depicted in the poetry of the era, the tone was not unduly disrespectful. But it is clear that the black/white symbolic associations were being implanted, the color black representing tragedy, ugliness, and evil, while white connoted purity, beauty and goodness.

According to the Hispanist Miriam DeCosta, valuable information about the Spanish perception of blacks, both slaves and non-slaves, can be gained from the study of Spanish medieval church murals, paintings, and illuminated manuscripts, especially those illuminations contained in the *Càntigas de Santa Maria* (Poems about the Virgin Mary), a collection of some 420 poems by Alfonso X "the Wise" (1220-1284), king of Christian Spain.[4] These poems, which glorify the miracles performed by the Virgin Mary, include some which portray Moorish women. Alfonso X equates blackness with ugliness when he writes:

Non quer eu donzela fea,	I do not want an ugly maiden,
e negra come carbon.[5]	black as coal.

In another medieval text, *El Caballero Cifar* (The Knight Named Cifar), the oldest original romance of chivalry, probably written between 1299 and 1305, the theme of Africa is present and there are descriptions of the misadventures of various Moorish kings to exemplify the evils of avarice.[6]

In the next century, Luis Monguio finds that given the presence of numerous blacks in Spain, their rather frequent portrayal in the *cancionero* poems of the period is to be expected. Thus, two of the most prolific poets, Juan Álvarez Gato and Pedro de Cartagena, mention them in their verses, the former as a point of departure for a comic-affective comparison and the latter for purposes of a burlesque comparison as an example of ugliness.[7]

The situation changes during the Spanish Renaissance (1474-1556). Throughout this period there is hardly a single example of the literary presence of blacks in Spain. Monguio explains the absence of blacks as probably the result of the Renaissance poet's obsession with an ideal beauty and his refusal to pay attention to blacks who were atypical in a white world. Monguio notes that references to blacks are found only in satirical poems. He gives as an example Don Diego de Hurtado (1503-1575), who in a satirical poem in praise of ugliness suggests *la dama negra* (the black woman) as the prototype.[8]

The dearth of literary allusions to black men and women which characterizes the lyric poetry of the Spanish Renaissance is not duplicated in traditional folk poetry of the 16th and 17th centuries. References to blacks, especially the *morena* (dark-skinned woman), abound in traditional folk poetry, which sometimes apologizes for her skin color but more often praises her beauty. In various instances, the poetry reflects what Bruce Wardropper describes as the "neurosis of the *morena*."[9] He finds this "neurosis" to be born of the frustrations of being a dark-skinned woman in a society whose ideal beauty is blonde-haired and green-eyed.[10] In this poetry, the *morena* often laments the color of her skin and considers herself unattractive and unable to attract a suitable husband. In other poems, the *morena* attempts to justify her "defective" coloring. Typical excuses include the reference to too much time spent in the sun:

Morenica me llaman,	They call me little dark girl,
blanca nací,	but I was born white.
el sol del enverano	The summer sun
me puso así.[11]	made me like this.

The same theme appears in Lope de Vega's *El gran duque de Moscovia* (The Grand Duke of Muscovy):

Blanca m'era yo	I was white
cuando entré en la siega;	when I went to work in the fields;
diome el sol	the sun shone on me
y ya soy morena.[12]	and now I'm dark.

In a poem from Sebastián de Horozco's *Cancionero* (Anthology), the *morena* blames the rigors of country life for her ugliness and for the darkness of her skin:

Crième en la aldea,	I was raised in the country,
hiceme morena;	and it made me brown;
si en villa me criara,	if I had been in the city,
más bonica fuera.[13]	I would have been prettier.

The *morena* who sings the following ballad also notes that she was born white but farm life has changed her color:

Aunque soi morena	Though I'm dark now
blanca io nací,	I was born white,
guardando el ganado	by tending the cattle
la color perdi.[14]	I lost my color.

Exposure to the sun and other natural elements and the harsh life of the farm constitute frequent apologies for darkness, which continues to be synonymous with ugliness and undesirability. Yet another recourse is to blame her dark skin on bad luck and suffering as in this ballad from Alonso de Ledesma (1562-1623):

Duelos me hicieron negra,	Suffering made me black,
que yo blanca me era.[15]	for I used to be white.

Despite the severity of the plight of the *morena*, there was available to her the consolation derived from the example of the Virgin Mary depicted in traditional folk poetry as a *morena*, albeit "a special kind of *morena*, exempted by special privilege from contamination by color as she had been exempted from all contamination by the sin the color represents."[16]

This example from the *Cancionero de Upsala* (1556) is often cited:

Yo me soy la morenica,	I am a little *morena*,
yo me soy la morena.	a little *morena* am I.
Lo moreno bien mirado	They say the color brown
fué la culpa del pecado,	was the source of the sin,
que en mi nunca fué hallado	but I have never been bad,
ni jamás se hallará.	nor will I ever be.
Soy la sin espina rosa,	I am the thornless rose,
que Salomón canta y glosa,	whom Solomon praises,
nigra sum sed formosa,	"I am black but comely,"
y por mí se cantará,	and they sing my praises,
Yo soy la mata inflamada	I am the burning bush
ardiendo sin ser quemada,	burning but unscathed,
ni de aquel fuego tocada	untouched by the flame
que a los otros tocará.[17]	which will engulf the others.

Traditional folk poetry also offers the example of the *morena* of praiseworthy beauty. This poetry uses as a point of departure, in defense of the *morena*, the text from the Old Testament "Nigra sum, sed formosa" ("I am black, but comely").[18] No longer is there an apologetic note when praising the *morena*, nor does she offer excuses for her dark skin. Instead, there is a preference on the part of the *morena* to be addressed as such and not euphemistically:

> No me llames
> sega la erva
> sino morena.[19]

> Don't say
> that I'm the color of wheat,
> call me *morena*.

José María Alín sees the 16th-century *villancicos* (popular dance-songs) of Juan Vásquez as initiators of this newly expressed posture lauding the beauty of the *morena*. In this example, from Vásquez, the *morena* assumes an attitude of defiance:

> Aunque soy morenica y prieta
> a mí qué se me da,
> que amor tengo
> que me servirá.[20]

> Although I'm brunette and dark
> what does it matter to me,
> for I am loved,
> and that's enough for me.

In some of the poems, it is the lover who seeks to console his *morena* by reassuring her that he loves her color:

> No tengáis pasión, señora,
> en ser morena,
> que morena es la color
> que a mí da pena.[21]

> Don't be ashamed, madam,
> of being brown,
> for brown is the color
> which I love.

> Ábalos tus ojos,
> linda morena,
> ábalos, ábalos,
> que me dan pena![22]

> Lower your eyes,
> pretty brown woman,
> lower them, lower them,
> for they wound my heart.

Her brown skin becomes the symbol of *la buena color* (the good color) in this poem from Baptista Montidea's *Cancionero*:

> No desprecies, morenica,
> la tu color tan morena,
> que esa es la color buena.
> Ya se ha dado por sentencia
> que el moreno es más preciado,
> y en tu rostro delicado
> tiene muy mejor presencia.
> Del moreno y su apariencia,
> perla, no tengas pena,
> que esa es la color buena.[23]

> Do not belittle, brown girl,
> your dark brown color,
> for that is the good color.
> It is an accepted fact
> that brown is more highly valued,
> and on your delicate face
> it looks even prettier.
> Do not worry, dearest,
> about how brown skin looks,
> for it is the best color.

Little by little, the *morena* imposed her color, until finally in the 17th century more folk poems were devoted to her than to her white counterpart.[24] The *morena* becomes the object of sincere love and deep passion.[25] Here the lover has surrendered his love to her:

Tengan, tengan, señores	Gentlemen, grab her,
essa morena,	grab that *morena*,
ténganla que malleba	stop her for she's taking
mi amor tras ella.[26]	my heart with her.

And here the lover expresses his distress at the thought of losing his *morena*:

No huyas, morena	Don't leave me, *morena*,
duélete de mí,	have pity on me,
que no sé que tengo	for I've not been myself
después que te vi.[27]	since I first saw you.

While the *morena* became a thematic constant in traditional folk poetry of the 16th and 17th centuries, her darker sister, the *negra*, is portrayed with greater frequency in the theater by the *entremés* writers: Juan de Timoneda (d. 1583), Miguel de Cervantes (1547-1616), Luis Quiñones de Benavente (1589?-1651), Diego Sánchez de Badajoz, who wrote between 1533 and 1599, Simón Aguado, Francisco de Avellaneda (1622-?), Pedro Calderón de la Barca (1600-1681), and most notably Lope de Rueda (1510?-1565), who in his *comedias* and *pasos* gives the *negra* a more humanized and multifaceted treatment than do some of his contemporaries.

Much of Lope de Rueda's success in the theater depends on his skillful use of black female characters to incorporate popular and realistic elements into his *comedias* and *pasos*.[28] The *pasos*, short scenes or interludes which depict an event from everyday life to provide comic relief, also provide an especially appropriate vehicle for the picturesque portrayal of West Indian and African women who are variously jovial, pretentious, loquacious, vulnerable, and vulgar.[29] Lope's *negras* include Fulgencia in the *Diálogo de Timbria* (Tymbria's Dialogue), the maid Eulalia in *Eufamia*, and Guiomar, the maid of Clavela in *Los engañados* (The Deceived Ones).

In a scene from *Eufamia*, the maid Eulalia appears with her suitor, Polo. Although she is suffering from a harsh chemical with which she has sought to bleach her hair, she insists on finding a whitening agent for her hands. Polo attempts to dissuade her by expressing his love for her and his satisfaction with her color:[30]

Eulalia:
Assí la verdad, que aunque tengo	To tell the truth, though
la cara morenica, la cuerpo tengo	my face is dark, my body
como un terciopelo dobles.	is like velvet.

Polo:
A ser más blanca, no valías nada.   If you were fairer, I
Adió, que assí te quiero para   could not love you more.
hazer reales.³¹   I love you as you are.

The *pasos* of Lope de Rueda were forerunners of the *entremés*, a one-act humorous or satirical play or skit which was presented between the acts of a longer play in the Golden Age theater. The *entremés* attracted the dramatic talents of both major and minor playwrights of the 16th and 17th centuries. The black character, generally depicted as a comic figure, is a favorite type of many writers of this short dramatic form. Much of the comic value of these characterizations depends on the writers' use of the language of the Spanish blacks. Edmund de Chasca, while agreeing that the distortion of black speech patterns was used for comic effect in these early dramas, argues that "Rueda and his fellows reproduced the essential peculiarities of contemporary *Negro* speech."³²

The black female character appearing in the works of some *entremés* writers is typically described in her physical aspect with emphasis given to the color of her skin. Simón Aguado in his *Entremés de los negros* (The Blacks, 1602), describes the wedding between the *negrilla* (little black girl) Dominga, slave of Ruiz, and the *negro* Gaspar, slave of Rubio. These black characters use the *castellano deformado* (broken Spanish) which Juan R. Castellano, unlike Edmund de Chasca, considers as more of an invention of the *entremés* writers than a faithful reproduction of black speech.³³

Akin to Aguado's portrayal of Dominga is that of the black slave Francisca in the anonymous *entremés* titled *El Negro* (The Black Man). This slave girl evokes high praise from her owners, Don Luis and Doña Ana, who call her *un ángel de azabache* (a jet-black angel) and who, because of their devotion to her, arrange to marry her to a suitable black. Castellano provides this example of the bridegroom's boundless praise of his new wife:

Digo Francisquiya mía   Let me tell you, Francisca
que quiero vosa mesé   that I love you
como lanzorra las viñas   as a fox loves grapes,
como scribano los pleitos,   as a lawyer loves cases,
el tramposo las mentiras   as a slickster loves lies,
el médico los enfermos...³⁴   as a doctor loves sick people...

A great poet and playwright of the Spanish Golden Age, Lope de Vega (1562-1635), likewise frequently features blacks in his dramatic works. On occasion these black characters occupy important roles. Lope presents a diverse perspective of his black characters, who are often domestic servants working in the households of Spanish aristocratic families. Some of these servants are mistreated, while others enjoy a more favored and respected position, sometimes acting as confidantes. Lope also describes, in full detail, love affairs between the servants and the love interests which developed between the black servants and their masters and mistresses.[35]

Lope de Vega also depicts the lives of blacks in the New World: their laughter, their music, their dances, and the harsh realities of their day-to-day existence. Mónica Mansour finds that Lope always presents blacks as human beings, achieving a complete vision by the creation of three types of plays: those in which the white employer complains about his black servants, insults them and refers to them using the derogatory epithets which were then in vogue; those in which the whites recognize the humanity of their black servants; and those in which the *mulata* or the *negra* is presented as the ideal of beauty, the quality of which is affirmed by all, including the woman herself.[36]

Mansour attributes much of the literary "dignification" of blacks to Lope de Vega.[37] An earlier assessment made by Carter G. Woodson in his study "Attitudes of the Iberian Peninsula (In Literature)," though somewhat less sweeping than that of Mansour, expresses a similar conviction: "Lope de Vega brought the Negro into his writings . . . without prejudice. He frequently referred to black saints and occasionally played up persons of color in his comedies . . . . Lope de Vega had a fondness for Negro music and dance, and . . . frequently introduced black characters to dramatize the achievements of the race in these spheres."[38]

Among the black characters introduced by Lope de Vega in his theater were "fascinating mulatto women, among whom the enamored cleric found perhaps one of his dearest sweethearts and admired her flesh the color of quince . . . ."[39] Although the noted Cuban scholar Fernando Ortiz refers to the "fascinating mulatto women" which comprised Lope's theatrical and personal repertoire, there seem to be black women of all shades in Lope's work and even a preference for portraying the *negra*. The princess Sofonisba, mother of the black prince Antiobo in *El negro del mejor amo* (The Slave of the Best Master) is black; the queen who accompanied Melchor in *El mayor rey de los reyes* (King of Kings) is black; so are the female singers in *La victoria de la honra* (The Triumph of Honor) and the maid Lucrecia in *Capellán de la Virgen* (The Chaplain of the Virgin). However, there seems to be some evidence that the blacks themselves, during Lope's time, showed a preference for the euphemistic adjective *moreno*.[40]

Lope de Vega receives credit for presenting some new concepts of the *negra* in the theater. Raymond S. Sayers points out that Lope's black women "are no longer objects of laughter . . . but instead females who are very much courted and desired."[41] As an example, he cites the mulatto slave in Lope de Vega's play *Amar, servir y esperar* (To Love, Serve and Wait):

una esclava mulatilla,	a little mulatto slave,
de semblante socarrón,	with a cunning look,
que ya sabes que estas son	for you know that they are
los lunares de Sevilla,	the moles of Seville,
sin envidiar el marfil,	without envy of marble,
la tez de ébano, lustrosa	their lustrous ebony skin,

más limpia y más olorosa	cleaner and more fragrant
que flor de almendro en abril...[42]	than almond blossoms in spring...

Pedro Calderón de la Barca (1600-1681), another of Spain's great Golden Age dramatists, also projects blacks onto his stage where, according to Woodson, they benefit from a more favorable treatment than previously.[43] In Calderón's drama *Sabila del oriente y gran reina de Sabá* (Sabila of the Orient and the Great Queen of Sheba), among the black characters figure the women Irife, Casimira, and Irene. In another of his plays, *Los hijos de la fortuna, Teágenes and Cariclea* (The Children of Fortune, Teagenes and Cariclea), Persina, the black queen of Ethiopia, abandons her newborn daughter, Cariclea, whose skin is too fair.

From Lope de Rueda to Pedro Calderón de la Barca, the theater of the Spanish Golden Age provides many references to the black woman, sometimes *mulata*, other times *negra*, and occasionally *morena*. Black women continue to be portrayed as humorous characters, but they are shown more realistically and given more individuality and humanity than in earlier Spanish literature.[44]

According to Fernando Ortiz, blacks in the Spanish theater of the Golden Age were more than characters in the plot; they were also actors and authors who contributed to the Spanish theater some of its most typical forms, such as the short comic dramatic sketch known as the *mojiganga* and the comic actor, the *bululú*. The *mojiganga* and the *bululú* are "essentially Negro creations, by their names, content and style, Castilian adaptations of the primitive African theater, which the mulatto artists inherited from their Negro ancestors and transported by the ingenuity of their dramatic art into the language of their white ancestors and to the Spanish theater."[45]

Blacks were treated very differently in Spanish theater and poetry. Mansour attributes this to the fact that the theater creates its black characters, inspired directly from reality, while poetry adopts them from the theater after they have already been converted into literary personages.[46] Therefore, a closer proximity is apparent between the real black and the dramatic character, than between the actual black person and the black as he is portrayed in poetry, where he is more stylized and many times a mere symbol.[47] This process is found throughout the history of the black in Spanish literature.[48]

Whereas the lyric poets of the Spanish Renaissance largely ignored the black presence, the lyric poets of 17th-century Spanish Baroque capitalized on black themes and black personae. In the poetry of Francisco de Quevedo (1580-1645), Luis de Góngora (1561-1627), and the minor Baroque poets, blacks are the objects of burlesque or satiric treatment. As in the Spanish theater, much of the comedy in this poetry is produced by the use of a black dialect. The poets likewise give full play to the superstitions and prejudices which existed against blacks and their physical appearance.[49]

The figure of a black bride occurs in the *Boda de negros* (A Black Wedding) by Quevedo. This 13-stanza poem identifies gloom with the color black, a phenomenon which, according to Mansour and others, is evident as far back as Hispano-Arabic texts:⁵⁰

Vi, debe de haber tres días,	About three days ago, I saw
en las gradas de San Pedro	on the hills of San Pedro
una tenebrosa boda,	a gloomy wedding,
porque era toda de negros.⁵¹	because it was all black.

Quevedo's first mention of the principals of this "gloomy" wedding ceremony appears in the following stanza:

Parecía matrimonio	It looked like a marriage
concertado en el infierno:	arranged in Hell:
negro esposo y negra esposa	a black groom and black bride
y negro acompañamiento.⁵²	and a black wedding party.

In this poem, which was published in *Romances varios* in 1643, the poet extends his caricature of the black bride:

Iba afeitada la novia	The bride came along
todo el tapetado gesto,	with her dark brown face,
con hollín y con carbón	adorned with soot and coal
y con tinta de sombreros.⁵³	and jet black dye.

Despite the disgust and mockery with which he depicts the protagonists and events of this black wedding, Martha Cobb discovers a certain ambivalence in his treatment of blacks. She points out that while in his *Boda de negros* he "exaggerates and burlesques the Blackness of a wedding party, the gestures and manners of the participants to the point of making fun of them, ridiculing their Blackness, on the other hand, in his *La Hora de Todos* (A Time for All People), he expresses compassion for Black slaves in their unfortunate condition."⁵⁴ Further, in contrast to the caricature of the black *novia* (bride) in *Boda de negros*, Miriam DeCosta finds that in the prose piece *La Hora de Todos*, "black women are flatteringly characterized as *hermosas a oscuras* (hidden/dark beauties)."⁵⁵

For the critic Lemuel Johnson, it is not the blacks created by Quevedo who represent the most consistent example of caricature in Spanish Baroque poetry, but rather those invented by another noted poet of the period, Luis de Góngora, who composed various poems about blacks, including "En la fiesta del Santísimo Sacramento" (The Feast of the Holy Sacrament), "El Nacimiento de Cristo Nuestro Señor" (The Birth of Christ Our Lord), "Por una negra señora" (For a Black Lady), and "En la fiesta de la adoración de los Reyes" (On the Feast of the Adoration of the Kings).⁵⁶

In Góngora's "En la fiesta del Santísimo Sacramento", two *morenicas*, Juana and Clara, prepare for the celebration of the festival of Corpus Christi:

Juana:
Mañana es Corpus Cristi
mana Crara;
Alcoholémono la cara
e lavémono la vista.

Clara:
¡Ay, Jesú, cómo sa mu trista!

Juana:
¿Qué tiene, pringa señora?

Clara:
Samo negra pecadora
e branca la Sacramenta.

Juana:
La alma sá como la denta
Crara mana.
Pongamo fustana
e bailemo alegra;
que aunque samo negra,
sa hermosa tú.[57]

Tomorrow is Corpus Christa
sister Clara;
let's put alcohol on our faces
and wash them very well.

Oh, Jesus, I'm so sad!

What's wrong, brown-skinned lady?

We are black sinners
and the Sacrament is white.

Our souls are as white as pearls,
Clara, my sister.
Let's get all dressed up
and dance gaily,
for though we're black,
we are pretty.

Juana and Clara represent Góngora's contribution to and perpetuation of the stereotypical female "bembón" or "bozal" with their characteristic speech in broken Spanish. This linguistic recourse was borrowed from the theater of Lope de Rueda and Lope de Vega. In addition to the comic effect produced by defective speech of the blacks, Sylvia Wynter notes that "the figurative language of the poem, the black/white antithesis, responds to the lyrical despair of Clara (note the name) who, in rejecting the color black as an anti-symbol of the Sacrament, rejects herself."[58]

slave Blásica tries to console her friend Cristina by referring to the Virgin Mary who gained her freedom by becoming a slave of God. The portrayal of the Virgin Mary as a *morena* and as a slave of God is a motif which had appeared in Peninsular Spanish folk poetry of the 16th century. In utilizing this motif, Sor Juana affirms the notion of the Virgin Mary as a source of consolation for the black slave.

Sor Juana describes the attitude of the slaves to the Catholic religion: it promises much and provides very little. In her poem, "San Pedro Nolasco" (Saint Pedro Nolasco), this theme is further developed. A slave laments, in broken Spanish, the fact that the Virgin promises to redeem believers, but discriminates against black people:

La otra noche con mi conga	The other night with my black
turo sin durmi pensaba	woman,
que no quiele gente plieta	unable to sleep, I kept thinking
como eya so gente branca.[63]	that she doesn't like blacks
	because she is white.

Sor Juana's blacks always "speak in broken Spanish. Nevertheless, one notices a considerable lack of uniformity, not only between poems of different dates, but sometimes also in the same poem. But in general, it seems that the accent is not stylized and comes very close to a realistic reproduction."[64]

A contemporary of Sor Juana Inés de la Cruz, the Peruvian poet Juan del Valle de Caivedes (1652-1692), depicts blacks and mulattos in his *Diente de Parnaso* (The Fangs of Parnassus). This type of poem, which Monguio describes as *poesia de escarnio* (burlesque poetry), enjoyed a certain vogue in 17th-century Spain. In *Diente del Parnaso*, the blacks of Peru are not singled out for burlesque treatment, but rather they receive the same attention as the rest of the society of Lima.[65] Mansour credits the works of Juan del Valle de Caivedes with revealing the underpriviledged position of blacks in Lima society and the opinion that society held of them. Blacks and mulattos are treated as objects to be manipulated, and this same attitude pervades the poet's literary treatment of women—black, mulatto, and Indian.[66]

The following fragment of Juan de Caivedes' "Pregón" (Cry of the Vendor) clearly illustrates the objectification/dehumanization process which the non-white woman suffers at the hands of the Peruvian poet. Here, female quadroons, mulattos, blacks, and Indians are assigned a value which decreases as the depth of color increases:

Manda que las cuarteronas	Let it be that quadroons
tengan sin tasa el valor	be conferred immeasurable value
porque todo lo trigueño	because everything wheat-colored
anda caro el dia de hoy.	is very precious these days.

II. *Negras, Morenas,* and *Mulatas* in New World Spanish Literature: From the Poetry of the Colonial Period to the Twentieth Century

To continue an examination of black women in Hispanic literature, it becomes necessary to proceed to the Americas, where one can begin to trace the early appearances of black women in the mostly religious poetry of the 17th-century Mexican nun Sor Juana Inés de la Cruz. Born Juana Ramirez in the Viceroyalty of New Spain, Sor Juana generally receives credit for being the first writer to treat the black theme in Hispanic-American literature. Her *villancicos* (popular dance-songs) recount experiences from a childhood spent at her grandfather's ranch, where she had contact with black slaves who spoke of magic and sang their rhythmical songs to her.[59] Juana herself was the owner of a slave girl also named Juana, who was given to her by her mother. The slave Juana became a source of information and inspiration for the poet.

In 1679, when Sor Juana introduced her religious *villancico*, with its reference to two black princesses from Guinea—two female representatives of the dreaded black element of the society of New Spain—it was considered an audacious act.[60] It appears that the Mexicans of Sor Juana's era lived in constant fear of slave uprisings like those which occurred in the 16th century, when blacks constituted a large percentage of the total population.

Sor Juana's two black princesses, Blásica and Cristina, are street vendors of beans and yams. They decide to abandon their trade for the day in order to participate in the religious celebration. The poem describes them as they approach the church where the festivities are under way:

A la voz del sacristán	Hearing the sacristan's voice
en la iglesia se colaron	in the church, there approached
dos Princesas de Guinea	two princesses from Guinea
con bultos azabachados.	with jet black forms.
Y mirando tanta fiesta	And seeing so much celebrating
por ayudarla cantando	and to join in the singing,
soltando los cestos dieron	they put down their baskets,
albricias a los muchachos.[61]	to the delight of the young men.

Although these two princesses sing gaily while joining in the festivities, Sor Juana does not ignore the fact that they are slaves and, as suggested by Concha Meléndez, there is an element of protest, albeit veiled, against the conditions endured by the slaves in the Viceroyalty of New Spain.[62] The

Lo moreno lo hizo Dios	God made the color brown,
lo blanco, lo hizo un platero	a silversmith made white;
como mi vida es morena	my life is brown, since
por una morena muero. (p. 134)[74]	I'm dying of love for a *morena*.

In her defense of her color, the *morena* in this *copla* (ballad) from *Cantares tradicionales del Tucumán* (Traditional Ballads from Tucuman) recaptures a motif from 16th-century Spanish traditional poetry:

Morenita soy, señores	I am a *morena*, gentlemen,
morena del Tucumán;	a *morena* from Tucuman;
así, moreno, es el trigo	although wheat is brown
pero blanco sale el pan. (p. 144)	the bread turns out white.

In the following Argentine poem, however, the *negra* seems to be praised for her beauty:

Linda mi negra querida,	My pretty beloved *negra*,
¿dónde estará?	where can she be?
Si me tendrá en la memoria	Does she remember me
o me había olvidado ya. (p. 103)	or has she already forgotten me?

Here the lover contemplates and admires the black woman's curly hair:

Los cabellos de mi negra	My black girl's hair
son crespos y muy crespitos,	is curly, very curly,
y le forman en la cara	and it frames her face
racimitos, racimitos. (p. 133)	in little clusters.

Also present in Argentine folk poetry is the motif of the anxious lover who fears that his beloved *negra* will abandon him:

No puedo vivir sin ti,	I can't live without you,
y no te puedo olvidar:	and I can't forget you:
buena pena la que tengo;	I am truly suffering;
mi negra, ¿por qué te vas?	*Negra*, why are you leaving?
(p. 124)	

In this instance, the anxious lover foresees the day when his *negra* will desert him:

Arriba de aquellas sierras	High up in those hills,
tengo una casita de piedras,	I have a little stone hut,
pa irme a vivir solito	where I'll go to live alone
cuando me deje mi negra. (p. 125)	when my *negra* leaves me.

> Manda que negras e indias,
> pues harto bellacas son,
> valgan al precio que quieran
> de palo, patata o coz.[67]

> Let it be that blacks and Indians,
> being as roguish as they are,
> be worth whatever price they ask
> in beatings or kicks.

Some 100 years later, a Spanish poet living and writing in Peru, Esteban de Terrala y Landa, known as Simón Ayanque, continued the burlesque tradition of Caivedes in his work *Lima por dentro y fuera* (Lima Inside and Out) of 1797. Throughout this work, there are allusions to blacks and mulattos of whom, according to Leslie Rout, there were perhaps 130,000 living in the Viceroyalty of Peru.[68] Ayanque describes the black women who served as cooks and the mulattos who served as maids for the Peruvian gentry. Ayanque criticizes black women along with the rest of Lima society, which he depicts as gluttonous, deceitful, and peevish.[69]

Mansour points out another poem by Ayanque which provides information and insight into the inferior social and economic condition of blacks in late 18th-century and early 19th-century Lima: *Testamento codicilo, Última voluntad disposición testamentaria otorgada por un pobre que ya se cansó de serlo, y huyendo del Mundo, Demonio y Carne se quiere morir por no ver muchas cosas* (The Last Will and Testament of a Wretch, Tired of his Condition, who, Fleeing from the World, the Devil and Flesh, Wants to Die and not Witness so Many Things). According to Mansour, it seems that the white Peruvian, no matter how poor, felt superior to the black man—a superiority based solely on the color of his skin.[70]

Poetic references to black women are infrequent in the literature of the 18th century, in both Spain and the Americas. The situation, however, changes dramatically in the 19th century in Spanish America with an increase in the frequency of her appearance in the folk poetry of Argentina, Ecuador, Colombia, Venezuela, Mexico, Santo Domingo, and Cuba. The dark-skinned woman, whether *parda* (brown-skinned), *morena* (dark-skinned), *negra* (black), *mulata* (mulatto), *prieta* (black), or *trigueña* (wheat-colored), becomes a veritable source of inspiration for the folk poet.

José-Juan Arrom, in the chapter "Presencia del negro en la poesía folklórica americana" (Presence of Blacks in American Folk Poetry), organizes the vast poetic production of the epoch around four motifs: those poems which express sentiments of love, those which contain insults, those which defend or exalt black pride and dignity, and those which describe the gradual process from social inequality to acceptance.[71] Arrom further explains that amorous poems occur with greater frequency than the other types, and that there are few poems which insult the image of the black woman.[72] Insults, it seems, are reserved for the black males of those regions with the highest proportions of blacks in their population.[73]

In the folk poetry of Argentina, there is a preference for the use of *negra* when referring to black women. There are few poems in which the woman is referred to or refers to herself as *morena*. The following is one such exception:

The folk poetry of Ecuador offers examples of the suffering lover, the proud lover, and the defensive lover. Here the lover suffers at the hands of his *negra*:

Negrita Dolores,	*Negrita* Dolores,
dolores me das,	you make me suffer,
dolores, regalas,	you offer only pain,
dolores, no más. (p. 126)	pain and nothing more.

There is a hint of the Spanish courtly love tradition in this portrayal of the lover as slave, in this example from Ecuador:

A mi negrita yo adoro;	I adore my little *negra*;
mi dicha alabo,	I praise my good luck,
pues siendo ella la negra,	although she's the one who's black,
yo soy su esclavo. (pp. 134-35)	I am her slave.

The following poems from Ecuador assume a defensive posture on the part of the suitor who feels compelled to defend his attraction and love for his *negra*:

Dicen que la tierra negra	They say that black soil
da muy buena sementera;	gives a rich harvest;
por eso he puesto los ojos	that's why I've set my sights
en una moza tan negra. (p. 152)	on such a black girl.

Apparent here is the defensive stance of the husband of a black woman who has a "white soul":

Me enamoré de una negra,	I fell in love with a black girl
y con ella me casé;	and I married her;
pues dentro del cuerpo negro	but in her black body
un alma blanca encontré. (p. 153)	I found a white soul.

The popular poetry of 19th-century Colombia variously refers to the black woman as *negra, mulata, morena,* and *pardita*. Not all poems express praise for her beauty or character; some insult her. In the following example, the poet alludes to her ugliness, which for him stems from her blackness, an analogy which has already been noted in the 13th-century poetry of Alfonso X:

Que fea que es una negra	How ugly is a black woman
vestida de muselina:	dressed up in muslin,
parece una raíz quemada	looking like a burnt root
con la ceniza pu' encima. (p. 136)	covered with ashes.

Conversely, in this poem from the region of Antioquia, Colombia, the value of the pretty *pardita* (brown-skinned girl) is extolled:

Vale más una pardita	A pretty brown-skinned girl
que una blanca siendo hermosa:	is better than a white one:
si la pardita es graciosa	and if she's charming too,
válgame Dios, qué cosita. (p. 135)	my, my, what a prize!

Also from Colombia, emanating from the region of Paitiá, the poet compares a black woman with natural phenomena:

De la peña vierte el agua,	Water flows from the rock,
del agua nace el pescado;	fish come from the sea;
de la boca de mi negra	from my *negra's* mouth
sale un clavel encarnado. (p. 126)	a red carnation appears.

A less exalted vision of the black woman is presented with some frequency in the folk poetry of Venezuela. For example:

Queriendo estuve a una negra	I was in love with a black woman
un verano y un invierno	one summer and one winter
y me parece que estuve	and it was just like being
diez años en el infierno. (p. 135)	ten years in Hell.

This example, however, also from Venezuela, demonstrates a certain delicacy in expressing amorous sentiment for the black woman:

Si la negra me diera	If my *negra* would give me
un suspiro de amor,	a sign of her love,
en su pecho pusiera	I would place on her breast
con mi mano una flor. (p. 128)	with my hand, a flower.

The following ballad, in dialogue form, comes out of the Mexican tradition of folk poetry devoted to the theme of the black woman. Here the *negrita* responds monosyllabically, and with coy reserve, to her lover's inquiries:

¿Estamos solitos? - Si	Are we alone? - Yes
¿Y nadie nos oye? - No	And no one can hear us? - No
¿Quién es tu cielito? - Tú	Who is your love? - You
¿Quién es mi negrita? - Yo (p. 129)	Who is my *negrita*? - Me

Mexican folk poetry also offers this poem, in which the lover complains of his burdensome life with his black woman:

Para qué quiero cruces	Why do I need crosses
en mi rosario,	on my rosary,
si con mi negra tengo	when with my black woman
cruz y calvario. (p. 136)	I have both cross and Calvary.

Similarly, the popular poetry of Cuba teems with allusions to the *mulata* or *mulatica* and sometimes to the *negra* or *negrita*. In these poems, the woman's beauty captures the poet's attention:

Los ojos de mi mulata	My mulatto's eyes
luceros del alma son;	are my soul's stars;
al fulgor de sus destellos	my heart is inspired
se inspira mi corazón. (p. 130)	by their bright sparks.

The description of her peerless attractiveness is achieved by the use of imagery related to sugar and its properties:

No hay mulata más hermosa	There is no prettier mulatto
más pilla y más sandunguera	more clever and more exiting
ni que tenga en la cadera	or whose hips are sweeter
más azúcar que mi Rosa. (p. 130)	than my Rosa's.

The 19th-century literary view of the black woman is not limited to her portrayal in the folk poetry of various countries of Latin America, but also finds expression in the Romantic literature of the period. Latin American novelists and lyric poets manifested a sustained interest in black themes, and it is precisely in the romantic literature that blacks, both men and women, emerge with more frequency than previously as fictional and poetic protagonists. This was especially true of the Cuban novelists of the period, among them, Gertrudis Gómez de Avellaneda (1814-1873), author of *Sab*; Cirilo Villaverde (1812-1894), author of *Cecilia Valdés*; and Anselmo Suárez y Romero (1818-1878), author of *Francisco*. To a lesser degree black themes were treated in the novels of other Latin American writers. One such example is Jorge Isaacs (1837-1895) of Colombia in *María*.

In addition to the importance of novelists who used black themes or black characters in their works, various Cuban and Colombian poets helped create the literary foundation upon which 20th-century writers would elevate and perpetuate black literature. Chief among the poets who led the way are the Afro-Cuban "Plácido" (Gabriel de la Concepción Valdés, 1804-1844) and the Afro-Colombian Candelario Obeso (1849-1884), both of whom demonstrate a definite artistic interest in the portrayal of black women.

Plácido, a free Cuban mulatto who was executed in 1844 by the Spaniards for his alleged role in a slave uprising known as "Conspiración de la Escalera" (The Escalera Conspiracy), fashions a distinct image of black women. In the following poem, Plácido "celebrates the *mulata* with fresh conceits":[75]

Yo vi una veguera	I saw a country girl
trigueña, tostada	wheat-colored, so brown
que el sol, envidioso	that the sun, envious
de sus lindas gracias,	of her loveliness,
o quizá bajando	or perhaps descending
de su esfera sacra	from its lofty sphere

prendado de ella	smitten by her
le quemó la cara	burned her face
como el sol que abrasa	like a sun that toasts
en julio y agosto	in July and August
la flor de la caña.	the sugar cane blossom.
Veguera preciosa	Precious country girl
de la piel tostada,	with suntanned skin,
ten piedad del triste	have pity on this sad fellow
que tanto te ama;	who loves you so much;
mira que no puedo	you know I can't
vivir de esperanzas,	live on hopes,
sufriendo vaivenes	suffering ups and downs
como flor de caña.[76]	like a sugar cane blossom.

In 19th-century Colombian poetry, Candelario Obeso, like Plácido, demonstrates a genuine interest in the portrayal of black women who are indispensable to the happiness and sense of well-being of their mates. In his poem, "A mi morena" (To My Brown-Skinned Woman), the lover describes his sense of loss and sadness occasioned by the absence of his *morena*. In an attempt to persuade her to return, he enumerates the material benefits which she can expect to enjoy in his company:

Tengo lirio güeleroso	I have fragrant lilies
Y jamín de malabá;	and jasmine from Malabar.
En cosa re golosina	As for good eating
Tengo un grande nijperá,	I have a big persimmon tree,
Cocos, cirgüelo, naranjos,	coconuts, plums, oranges
Un no vijto platana...	and a splendid banana tree...
Tengo e toro, hata tabaco,	I have meat and even tobacco
Un ron que jace bailá,	and rum that'll make you dance.
Solo farta tu presencia	All I need is you
Pa ejte cielo acabalá.	to make my heaven complete.

Some controversy surrounds Obeso, whose role as a true precursor of black poetry is denied by Hortensia Ruiz del Vizo and championed by the critic Richard L. Jackson. Ruiz del Vizo maintains that Obeso's poetry does not have "any point of contact with today's black save the reproduction of the imperfect Spanish spoken by the black rowers."[77] However, Jackson argues that as early as 1877 Obeso "was according dignity to his black fellow countrymen while advising the local 'literati' that a truly national literary identity could be found only in local popular poetry and song. He believed the black man was a legitimate literary subject who should be presented authentically, talking his own language, expressing his own thoughts, and singing his own songs."[78]

The question of whether Cuban or Colombian poets are the true precursors of 20th-century black poetry may continue as an unresolved issue. But there is no question that 19th-century Cuban and Colombian writers, as well as their contemporaries in other Latin American countries, demonstrate a clear preoccupation with the description of black women. One such contemporary, Francisco Muñóz de Monte (1800-1868) of Santo Domingo, views the *mulata* as a voluptuous snake-like victimizer and destructive force. The snake is a symbol "frequently employed in the poetic description of the black woman. Many poets compare her movements with those of the serpent; she is the creature of sinuous and slithering gyrations, tantalizing the male. Other poets, influenced no doubt by the biblical fable, view the Afro-American woman as an evil despoiler of all that is good in man."[79] Muñóz combines these two somewhat different perceptions in his poem, "La mulata":

Cógelo entonces la gentil mulata
convulsiva, frenética, anhelante,
y en voluptuoso arrullo murmurante
su labio exhala la palabra amor.

The genteel mulatto seizes him
convulsive, frenetic, desirous,
and in a voluptuous murmuring
her mouth exhales the word love.

Y triunfa al exhalarla. El hombre es suyo,
el blanco le obedece servilmente;
en la boca fatal de la serpiente
el encumbrado pájaro cayó.[80]

And she triumphs as she speaks. The man is hers,
the white man obeys her slavishly;
in the fatal mouth of the serpent
the proud bird fell.

Like the poets Obeso, Plácido, and Muñóz, who lived and wrote during the Romantic period, the later Modernist poets also manifest a strong attraction to the black woman as literary subject. The outstanding figure of Modernism in Latin American literature, Rubén Darío (1867-1916), an Afro-Nicaraguan poet, creates a vision of the black woman as a sensual and exotic being. In his poem, "La negra Dominga" (The Black Girl Dominga), he produces an ambience with "words which insinuate rhythm, color, tropicalism, sensual words to be seen, heard, savored and felt":[81]

¿Conocéis a la negra Dominga?
Es retoño de cafre y mandinga,
es flor de ébano henchida de sol.
Ama el ocre y el rojo y el verde,
y en su boca, que besa y que muerde,
tiene el ansia del beso español.

Do you know the *negra* Dominga?
An offshoot of Kafir and Mandinga
an ebony flower filled with sunlight.
She loves yellow and red and green,
and her mouth, which kisses and bites,
yearns to savor the Spanish kiss.

Serpentina, fogosa y violenta,
con caricias de sal y pimienta
vibra y muestra su local pasión:
fuego que tiene Venus alaba
y envidiara la reina de Sabá
para el lecho del rey Salomón.

Serpentine, fiery and violent,
with caresses of honey and pepper,
she vibrates with wild passion:
an ardor which Venus praises
and which the Queen of Sheba
would desire for King Solomon's bed.

Vencedora, magnifica y fiera,	Victorious, magnificent and fierce,
con halagos de gata y pantera	with caresses of a cat or panther
tiende al blanco su abrazo febril,	she offers her feverish embrace to
y en su boca do el beso está loco,	the white man,
muestra dientes de carne de coco	and between her lips of wild kisses
con reflejos de lácteo marfil.[82]	flash her teeth of milky ivory.

Darío's poem is replete with negative stereotypical allusions that date back some three centuries to the era of Lope de Vega, when references to the black slave's color were typically used to produce a comic effect. The compliments of Lope's day, based on comparing a woman with the sun, ivory, and white flowers, were humorous when applied to a non-white subject. Equally comic was the result produced by praising the woman's blackness by comparing it with night, ebony, or a dark cloud—symbols which were so patently incongruous with the Spanish aesthetic. In his portrayal of the *negra* Dominga, Darío uses these black/white contrasts; she is an ebony flower filled with sunlight, i.e. darkness redeemed by light, and she is a panther salvaged by the ivory-like whiteness of her teeth.

A Mexican counterpart of Darío's image of the black woman can be found in the work of his contemporary, José Juan Tablada (1871-1945). Enrique Noble discovers in Tablada's "Canción de la mulata" (Song of the *Mulata*) traces of the fauna and flora "of the notoriety and psychographic hyperbole" associated with the myth of the mulatto woman, so characteristic of the 19th-century poems written on the same subject.[83]

Esos "que ven claro de noche," ¡vengan!	You "who see light in the dark," come!
¡Aquí hay candela!	Here you will find fire!
Mi cuerpo es una hamaca tropical con vaivén de danzón;	My body is a tropical hammock swaying to the rhythm of the *danzón*;
mis labios tienen miel de níspero;	my lips offer sweet honey;
mi cuerpo es un jardín nocturno;	my body is a nocturnal garden;
mis senos dos guanábanas;	my breasts two custard apples;
mis ojos dos cucuyos...	my eyes two glowworms...
Esos que mascan goma, vengan, ¡aquí hay candela!	You who chew gum, come, here you will find fire!
De la Reina de Sabá, Salomón amaba la candela;	Solomon loved the light of the Queen of Sheba;
vengan; para encenderse el corazón	come, I will give you fire
¡aquí hay candela![84]	to light up your hearts!

Tablada, who introduced the Japanese haiku to the Spanish language, uses this genre to present a black prostitute. His description, in the poem

"Jaikai", resorts to the traditional black/white contrast seen in Darío:

> Lágrimas que vertía
> La prostituta negra
> Blancas como las mías.[85]

> The tears that were shed
> by the black prostitute
> were as white as mine.

Another Mexican writer, Miguel N. Lira (b. 1905), novelist, playwright, critic, and poet, capitalizes on the attractiveness of the *negra* as dancer. In his poem "Rumba", the *negra* Rita's charms are so powerful that the surrender of the *negro* is inevitable:

> La negra gira en redondo
> y gira el negro bembón
> la negra baila los ojos
> y el negro su corazón.[86]

> The black girl whirls
> and her thick-lipped partner follows
> the black girl rolls her eyes
> and his heart pounds.

Rose E. Valdés-Cruz is quite correct in emphasizing the importance of the theme of the dancer in black poetry. She observes that the poets of this genre "feel a genuine delight in detailing with graphic expression the dancer's dress and kerchief, but they are more interested in her body: her eyes, arms, teeth, breasts; but, above all else, her hips and buttocks." She adds that while "white poetry prefers the pectoral curves and the pubic triangle, ...there is not a single creator of black poetry who has not been inspired to use gluteal metaphors."[87]

The black dancer reigns in 20th-century Cuban poetry. Titles such as "Bailadora de rumba" (Rumba Dancer) by Ramón Guirao (1908-1949), which appeared in 1928, and "La rumba" by José Z. Tallet (b. 1893), which presents the plasticity of the rumba dancer Tomasa, abound in Cuban poetry. Marcelino Arozarena (b. 1912) created the dancer Caridá, who, even though missing from the festivities, holds sway over her admirer, who asks repeatedly:

> ¿Por qué no viene a la bacha
> la hija de Yemayá,
> la pulposa,
> la sabrosa,
> la rumbosa y majadera Caridá?[88]

> Why doesn't the daughter of
> Yemaya come to the dance,
> the luscious,
> the charming,
> the elegant and spirited Carida?

In the case of María Belén Chacón, the absent dancer in "Elegía de María Belén Chacón" by Emilio Ballagas (1910-1954), so renowned and powerful is her artistry that the protagonist retains a vivid mental picture of her rhythmic movements:

> María Belén, María Belén:
> con tus nalgas en vaivén,
> de Camagüey a Santiago...
> de Santiago a Camagüey.[89]

> María Belén, María Belén,
> with your hips swinging,
> from Camagüey to Santiago...
> from Santiago to Camagüey.

The work of the noted Cuban mulatto poet Nicolás Guillén (b. 1902) presents a gallery of *negras* and *mulatas*. In his poetry one can trace at least three distinct attitudes vis-à-vis the black woman: an exaltation of her beauty in the traditional European mode, the subordination of her physical nature and glorification of her spiritual and intellectual qualities, and an unconditional acceptance and appreciation of her as a person. To illustrate Guillén's poetic postures, Kay Boulware offers as examples "Ana María" from the 1964 collection *Poemas de amor* (Love Poems), the poem "Angela Davis", written in 1971, and finally, "Mi chiquita" (My Little Woman) (1930).[90] What Boulware charts in "Ana Maria" "seems to be more in tune with traditional feminine descriptive poetry", i.e., the praise of European beauty:

> Ana Maria,
> la trenza que te cae
> sobre el pecho, me mira
> con ojos de serpiente
> desde tu piel torcida.[91]
>
> Ana Maria,
> your braid, falling
> over your breast, looks at
> me with a serpent's eyes
> from your undulating flesh.

In his poem to Angela Davis, Guillén subordinates the physical attributes of his subject to infer that she possesses more important intellectual and spiritual qualities:

> Yo no he venido aquí a decirte
> que eres bella,
> creo que sí, que eres bella,
> mas no se trata de eso.[92]
>
> I did not come here to say
> that you are beautiful.
> I know that you are beautiful,
> but it is not about that.

Boulware concludes by suggesting Guillén's poem "Mi chiquita" is an "exemplary contribution" to a certain unconditional poetic elevation and admiration for the black woman:

> La chiquita que yo tengo
> tan negra como é
> no la cambio po ninguna
> po ninguna otra mujé.[93]
>
> The girl that's mine
> as black as she is
> I wouldn't give her up
> for no other woman.

In Guillén's 1931 collection *Sóngoro Cosongo*, references to black women are found in the poems "Rumba", "Secuestro de la mujer de Antonio" (The Kidnapping of Antonio's Wife), and "Mujer nueva" (New Woman). In these poems, especially in "Mujer nueva", Constance Sparrow de García-Barrio sees the poet shaping the new feminine types and presenting these women as "belonging to a group from which little has been heard, but from which everything positive may now be expected."[94] Garcia-Barrio maintains that Guillén's new women represent an attempt to forge a vision of an "ideal woman".

Con el círculo ecuatorial	With the equatorial circle
ceñido a la cintura como	cinched to her waist as if
a un pequeño mundo,	to a small globe,
la negra, mujer nueva,	the black woman, a new woman,
avanza en su ligera bata de	advances in her sheer
serpiente.	serpent's robe.
Coronada de palmas,	Crowned with palms,
como una diosa recién llegada,	like a newly arrived goddess,
ella trae la palabra inédita,	she brings a sincere word,
el anca fuerte,	a strong back,
la voz, el diente, la mañana	her voice, her teeth, the morning
y el salto.[95]	and hope.

Before the Cubans Ramón Guirao, Emilio Ballagas, and Nicolás Guillén published their poems in the Afro-Cuban mode, the *poesía negra* (black poetry), or *poesía afroantillana* (Afro-Antillean poetry) of the Puerto Rican poet Luis Palés Matos (1899-1959) had appeared in Puerto Rico in various periodicals and had already received critical attention in Spain. The young critic José Robles Pazos praised Palés Matos in his article "Un poeta borinqueño" (A Puerto Rican Poet) published in "La Gaceta Literaria" (The Literary Gazette) of September 15, 1927.[96] In the year and a half prior to the publication of the Robles article, Palés Matos had written and published his poems "Africa," later renamed "Pueblo negro" (Black People), "Danza negra" (Black Dance), and "Danza canibal" (Wild Dance).

Palés Matos created his own original palette of *negras* and *mulatas* which includes, but is not limited to, the *mulata* Tembandumba de la Quimbamba in "Majestad negra" (Black Majesty), the *negra* of "Pueblo negro", and the *mulata* of "Mulata-Antilla" (Mulatto-Antilles).

Tembandumba de la Quimbamba, queen of the Carnival, is depicted in all of her candid sensuality in "Majestad negra":

Culipandeando la Reina avanza,	Swinging her hips the queen approaches
y de su inmensa grupa resbalan	and from her immense rump glide
meneos cachondos que el gongo cuaja	provocative wiggles which the drum converts
en ríos de azúcar y de melaza.	into rivers of sugar and molasses.
Prieto trapiche de sensual zafra,	Black mill of sensuous sugar cane,
el caderamen, masa con masa,	her hips, mass upon mass,
exprime ritmos, suda que sangra	squeeze out rhythms, exuding sweat,
y la molienda culmina en danza.[97]	and the grinding ends in a dance.

In "Mulata-Antilla", Palés Matos compares his mulatto woman with the fruits of his native tropical island—lemon, pineapple, sugar cane and custard apple. G.R. Coulthard notes that while it is traditional for European lyricism to compare the physical aspects of women with flowers, in substituting the names of local fruits there is an apparent shift in the attitude of the poet toward a blatant sensuality:[98]

Eres ahora, mulata,	You are now, mulatto girl,
todo el mar y la tierra de mis islas.	both the sea and land of my islands.
Sinfonía frutal cuyas escalas	A fruital symphony whose scales
rompen furiosamente en tu catinga.	erupt furiously in the smell of your body.
He aquí en su verde traje la guanábana	Here is the custard apple in its green dress,
con sus finas y blandas pantaletas de muselina, he aquí el caimito	with its delicate soft muslin pants. Here is the star-apple
con su leche infantil; he aquí la piña	with its childish milk; here is the pineapple,
con su corona de soprana...Todos los frutos ¡oh mulata! tú me brindas,	with its soprano crown...All these fruits, oh *mulata*, you offer me,
en la clara bahía de tu cuerpo por los soles del trópico bruñida.[99]	in the clear bay of your body browned by the tropical sun.

The black woman holds a special fascination for many of Palés Matos' compatriots—black, white, and mulatto. Even a cursory examination of Puerto Rican poetry suggests the preoccupation of these poets with Afro-Latin American women, the *negra*, and, more often, the *mulata*. The work of Luis Llorens Torres (1878-1944) offers an example in the sonnet "La negra" (The Black Woman). In his "Copla mulata", Llorens Torres portrays the woman:

Esta criolla pelinegra y ojinegra,	This black-haired, black-eyed
boquiroja y dientiblanca;	red-mouthed woman with white teeth;
esta cerrera, briosa,	this wild and spirited,
resollante potranca,	breathless filly,
temblorosa en el pecho,	with heaving chest
temblorosa en las ancas... (p. 13)[100]	and trembling buttocks...

Francisco Negroni Mattei (1896-1937) presents a portrait of a black woman in "Baila la negra el son" (The Black Girl Dances the *Son*) emphasizing her body as she dances the *son* to the rhythm of the *plena*. The work of Evaristo Ribera Chevremont (1896-1976), another of Puerto Rico's famous poets, includes the poem "Morena", which praises the beauty of the woman in these words:

Aguas peninsulares y caribes	Peninsular and Caribbean waters
descubren en sus conchas tu belleza... (p. 21)	discover your beauty in their shells...

Fortunato Vizcarrondo (b. 1896), author of the popular poem "Y tu abuela a' ónde ejtá?" (And Where's Your Grandmother?), in which one who pretends to be white is reminded by an associate that he has a black grandmother he keeps from the public eye, also wrote the poem "La mulata" dedicated to Carmen M. Colón Pellot (b. 1911).

Pero si no puedo ser	But if I can't be either
Negra, ni tampoco blanca... (p. 29)	black, or white...

Colón Pellot, herself a poet and journalist, is the author of the plaintive "Motivos de envidia mulata" (Thoughts on Mulatto Envy) in which the *mulata* covets the white cloud's freedom, admirers, etc.

A mí nadie me canta	No one sings my praises
a mí me esclavizan las normas;	all laws, Christian principles
las leyes cristianas.	enslave me.
....	....
Nadie busca mis risas morenas;	No one seeks my dark laughter;
nadie, nadie me idolatra,	nobody, nobody idolizes me,
aunque tengo la savia en mis copas	even though in my veins
burbujante y cálida. (p. 88)	the blood runs warm and bubbly.

Another Puerto Rican woman who explores the theme of the black woman is Julia de Burgos (1916-1953), acclaimed by Jorge Luis Morales as one of the greatest women poets of not only Puerto Rico but of all America.[101] Her poem "Ay, Ay, Ay de la grifa negra" (Lament of a Kinky-Haired Black Woman) begins:

Ay, ay, ay, que soy grifa y	Ay, ay, ay, I am pure black
pura negra;	with kinky hair;
grifería de mi pelo,	kinkiness in my hair,
cafrería en mis labios;	Kafir in my lips;
y mi chata nariz mozambiquea.	and my flat Mozambiquan nose.
Negra de intacto tinte,	A jet black woman
lloro y río	I cry and I laugh
la vibración de ser estatua negra;	about being a black statue,
de ser trozo de noche, en	about being a sliver of night,
que mis blancos	in which my white
dientes relampaguean... (p. 91)	teeth glisten...

Burgos expresses both the pain and the suffering of being black and appears to prefer to know that her ancestors were black slaves and not white slave owners.

Tomasita, the *negrita de la costa* (black girl from the coast) of Pedro Carrasquillo (1910-1954) describes herself:

> Soy la alegre Tomasita: | I am the happy Tomasita:
> güelfana, pobre y negrita | orphaned, poor and black
> pero, de güena calaña... (p. 84) | but of good character...

Tomasita dances the *rumba* and the *plena* and tells fortunes. Seña Chenchá, in the poem of the same name by the Puerto Rican poet Felipe Arana (1902-1962), is another fortune teller. An old, bald-headed black woman who wears a red bandanna, in addition to telling fortunes, she prepares magic potions:

> Es negra, descendiente de | She is black, descendant of
> rollizos. | sturdy stock.
> Teje esteras y sombreros de paja. | She weaves straw hats and mats.
> Lee los viernes la suerte | On Fridays, she reads the
> en la baraja, | cards,
> pega ventosas y prepara | and prepares her magic potions.
> hechizos. (p. 69)

Vicente Palés Matos (1903-1963) recalls his black "mammy" in the poem "La negra que me crió" (The Black Woman Who Raised Me):

> La vida entera he de acordarme | I will always remember
> de la negra que me crió: | the black woman who raised me:
> sus dulces ojos compasivos | her sweet loving eyes
> inclinados sobre el fogón, | turned towards the stove,
> el gordo seno que me daba, | her large breasts which fed me,
> y el delantal de calicó. (p. 70) | and her calico apron.

The poet describes his mourning for the dead *negra*:

> Todo el día estuve llorando | I cried all day long
> a la negra que me crió, | for the black woman who raised me,
> temiendo siempre que dijera | expecting to hear her say
> al ver mi llanto en el salón, | in her soft motherly voice,
> con su pastosa voz de madre: | on seeing me sobbing in the parlor:
> —Niño, pod Dioj...! (p. 71) | —Boy, what's wrong wid you?

III. *Negras*, *Morenas*, and *Mulatas* in the Contemporary Poetry of Peru, Uruguay, Ecuador, Venezuela and Colombia

In her treatment of the images of women in modern African poetry, Andrea Rushing offers the thesis that all images of African women are somehow related to the image of woman as mother. She insists that although African women have fulfilled other social roles, it is chiefly in their role as mother that they have achieved status and recognition. According to Rushing, "portraits of black women in African poetry seem to radiate from the Yoruba proverb 'Mother is gold'."[102] Such an understanding of the black woman in African poetry would shed light on her South American counterpart, especially as she is treated by black poets. Portrayals of the mother are rife in the 20th-century poetry by Afro-Latin American writers. She is seen and heard singing lullabies to her *negrito*; she functions as intercessor and interpreter in the supernatural realm in "La tunda para el negrito" (The Bogey Man for a Little Black Boy) by the Afro-Ecuadorian poet Adalberto Ortiz (b. 1914); and she appears gifted with knowledge that is superior to that of noted European scientists in "La infancia" (Childhood), by the white Venezuelan poet Miguel Otero Silva (b. 1908). Hers is the voice of the oppressed; her strength and endurance win praise such as that in the poems about Marimorena by the Afro-Uruguayan poet Virginia Brindis de Salas.

In the works of the Afro-Peruvian Nicomedes Santa Cruz (b. 1925), portraits of black women often criticize those who, like the bald-headed black woman in "Como has cambiado, Pelona" (My How You've Changed, Baldy), forget their African heritage and slavishly imitate their white mistresses. Other Santa Cruz portraits humorously depict the somewhat loose morals of a friend's wife. However, Santa Cruz takes on a deadly air of sobriety and almost awesome respect when he describes the mother or grandmother. In his "Día de la madre" (Mother's Day), he decries the notion of dedicating just one day a year to recognize and praise the mother:

Este domingo de mayo	This Sunday in May
vergüenza debiera darme:	should make me ashamed:
marcar un día del año	to single out one day of the year
para querer a la madre.[103]	to honor my mother.

To him, the mother merits constant homage and accolades:

> Pero me apena que exista
> sólo un "día de la madre"
> cuando toda una existencia
> no basta para adorarla.[104]

> It grieves me that only
> one day exists to honor our mothers
> when a whole lifetime
> would not suffice to pay her homage.

Similarly, in his portrayal of the Angolan grandmother in the title poem from his book, *Ritmos negros del Perú* (Black Rhythms of Peru), Nicomedes Santa Cruz lauds the strong woman who survived the journey across the Atlantic in a Spanish galley and the subsequent ill treatment by Spanish slaveowners.

> Y en América del Sur
> al golpe de sus dolores
> dieron los negros tambores
> ritmos de la esclavitud.[105]

> And in South America
> to the beat of her sufferings
> the black drums played
> slave rhythms.

The Afro-Uruguayan poet Pilar E. Barrios (b. 1889) joins Santa Cruz in defense and praise of the black woman as mother. In his "Poema de la madre" (Poem of the Mother), he asks rhetorically: "¿Influye en algo el color de la epidermis?" (Does her skin color somehow matter?)

For Barrios, the woman's function is to bear the next generation, and even when she has not yet contributed to the perpetuation of the race, he sees her as poised and waiting for motherhood:

> ...una mujer, cualquiera sea su raza
> desde que llega a la edad puberta
> es una madre en ciernes,
> antesala por cuya abierta puerta
> llegará un día el engendro.[106]

> ...a woman, whatever her race,
> from the time she attains puberty,
> is a mother-in-waiting,
> a foyer through whose open door
> a child will one day appear.

The Venezuelan poet Miguel Otero Silva, in the poignant memories of his childhood landscape, presents the black woman Marcolina in "La infancia", written in 1966:

> La negra Marcolina era cambiante
> y agorera como el mar.
> Había días tranquilos en que
> caminaba por la playa
> soledosa, llorando a su negrito
> muerto...[107]

> The black Marcolina was moody
> and clairvoyant, like the sea.
> There were calm days when she
> walked along the beach,
> lonely, mourning her dead black
> boy...

Marcolina, mother of the dead *negrito*, assumes a maternal relationship with the poet. She helps form his system of beliefs, his perception of the world:

Yo creía en San Miguel,	I believed in Saint Michael,
en los fantasmas,	in ghosts,
en las brujas.	in witches.
Como no iba a creer si la negra Marcolina	How could I not believe when the black Marcolina
me los había mostrado con su	had shown them to me with her
largo dedo de bejuco.[108]	long rattan finger.

"Quitandeira" by the Afro-Uruguayan poet Gastón Figueira (b. 1905), describes another maternal figure, a black woman from Bahia on the Brazilian coast. Like Miguel Otero Silva's Marcolina, Figueira's *negra* belongs to his childhood and is associated with the simple sweetness and innocence of his youth. For all her implicit maternity his *quitandeira* is a working woman, who earned a meager existence selling sweets in the street.

The *quitandeira* reminds us of another street vendor, Marimorena, the black woman fashioned by another Afro-Uruguayan poet, Virginia Brindis de Salas. One of the few women poets of Uruguay, Brindis de Salas depicts a variety of black women in her volume *Pregón de Marimorena* (Cry of Marimorena) while protesting the social and economic conditions of blacks in her native Uruguay. Marimorena, a black woman who carries bundles of newspapers which she offers for sale, can be seen in all manner of inclement conditions in "Pregón número dos" (Cry Number Two):

No hay sol que arredre nunca,	No amount of sun keeps you away,
ni lluvia que te aglutine;	nor does the rain drive you back,
y si se empapa tu nuca	and if you get sopping wet
o chapotean tus botines,	or your boots get soaked,
vas adelante y pregonando...[109]	you keep right on peddling...

In "Pregón número uno" (Cry Number One), only the poet seems to recognize and admire the vital contribution that Marimorena makes:

en cambio tú	on the other hand, you
pagas con creces;	pay dearly for
su periodismo	their journalism
su propaganda politiquera	their political propaganda,
todas sus lacras, su egoísmo	all their defects and selfishness,
sus fementidas torpes carreras.[110]	their false and dull careers.

Indeed, Marimorena seems to fulfill a function steeped in the traditional African feminine roles—that of merchant and, to some extent, bearer of news. Brindis de Salas conveys the importance of Marimorena's highly sophisticated manipulation of the language to sell her newspapers. But even more importantly, Brindis' portrayal links Marimorena to the vital African oral tradition, while contrasting it with the less vital European tradition of the written word. The poet asks:

¿Qué harían con el tiraje	What would become of their news
sin tu pregón solidario?[111]	without your sound support?

The poet relates the figure of Marimorena to the role of mother and grandmother when she laments in "Pregón número uno":

Tu voz, que nunca arrulló	Your voice, never singing lullabies
a tus hijos	to your children
ni a tus nietos	or your grandchildren—
y es voz de paria	a pariah's voice,
arrulla mimosamente	gently proffers
toda la prensa diaria.[112]	the daily newspaper.

The Colombian poet, Helcías Martán Góngora (b. 1920), presents a portrait of another black mother, this time a cigar-smoking great-grandmother. His portrayal is at once critical and sympathetic. His negative criticism derives from her pretensions and her apparent pride in her "Spanish" heritage. But as she smokes her *congola*, she hears "the flapping of the sails of the Spanish slave boat" that brought her to South America as human cargo. So great is the stigma of her African origin, that her descendants, even to the fourth generation, are accursed. In the poem "Blasón" (Family Coat of Arms), the great grandmother

carga y carga su congola	puffs and puffs her *congola*
mientras alguien, en la escuela,	while at the schoolhouse
pisa al biznieto la cola	someone steps on her grandson's tail
cuando orgulloso revela	when he speaks with pride
que tiene sangre española.[113]	of his Spanish blood.

In Martán Góngora's "Pejca" (Fishing), written in the language of blacks of Colombia, a black fisherman demonstrates his delight at the prospect of becoming a father by promising to the mother-to-be all manner of gifts:

Voy a pejcate la luna	I'm gonna catch you a moon
...Voy a pejcate un lucero	...I'm gonna catch you a morning star
...Er día que nazca mijo	...The day my son is born,
pa mojtrate er regocijo	to show you my delight,
er mar te voy a pejca...[114]	I'm gonna catch you the sea.

The white Venezuelan poet Andrés Eloy Blanco (1897-1955) portrays the grieving black mother Juana, whose little boy has just died. Hoping to find some consolation for her loss by entertaining the idea that at least her lost *negrito* will find a place in God's heaven, she is disenchanted by her friend's explanation that even in heaven there is discrimination against blacks and that there are no "little black angels" in heaven. The plaintive, angry plea of the black mother, Juana, is heard in Eloy Blanco's poem "Angelitos negros" (Little Black Angels):

Y entonces ¿adónde van angelitos de mi pueblo, zamuritos de Guaviare torditos de Barlovento?[115]	So tell me, where do the little angels from my town go, those black kids from Guaviare, those black kids from Barlovento?

The image of the mother—singing lullabies to comfort her *negritos*, not singing so that she can use her voice to peddle newspapers, interpreting the phenomena of the supernatural world, providing charming memories for the youth, or raising her voice in protest against the injustices of a racist heaven and earth—clearly surfaces as one of the dominant aspects of black women in 20th-century South American poetry. As might be expected, these portraits emerge almost exclusively from the pens of the black poets. As such, they stand slightly apart from the image of the dancer, which represents another central mold into which the black woman has been cast.

The portrayal of the black woman as a supersensual, spellbinding, and frenetic dancer of the *rumba, merengue, joropo,* or *cumbia*, so prevalent in the works of the late 19th- and early 20th-century Caribbean poets, continues to capture the imagination of the 20th-century Afro-South American poets. In their poetry, the dancing figure is variously admired for her vibrant, rhythmic movement, deplored and criticized for her primitive qualities, or praised for her closeness to African culture and for her contribution to the preservation of its meaning.

The Colombian poet Hugo Salazar Valdés (b. 1924), in his poem "Baile negro" (Black Dance), goes beyond the mere depiction of the sensual dance of the *negra*. He expresses a feeling of loathing for the drunken dance that she performs. He seems equally to deplore the origin of her sensual rhythm:

y entre los senos, boas perversas como en los ojos de la borrachera laten los perros de los ancestros y de los ritos de Africa negra.[116]	and within her breasts, perverse boas, as in her two drunken eyes the dogs of the ancestors and of black African rituals howl.

Arturo Camacho Ramirez (b. 1909), another Colombian poet, describes the wild dance of Bamba:

Bamba, atada a la noche, se tumba entre la sombra mordida por los sobrios tambores de la rumba.[117]	Bamba, chained to darkness, tumbles in the shadows seized by the somber drums of the *rumba*.

Here, the poet's disapproval is more restrained than that of his compatriot Hugo Salazar Valdés. Indeed, he suggests that there is a kind of mindlessness, even self-destructiveness, in the frenzied quality of Bamba's dance.

The Afro-Colombian poet Jorge Artel (b. 1909), encourages his *mulata* to dance, seeing in her a repository of African culture and value:

¡Danza, mulata, danza!	Dance, mulatto, dance!
En tus piernas veloces	In your agile legs
y en el son	and in the rhythm that
que han empapado tus lúbricas caderas,	embraces your smooth hips, the memory of two hundred
doscientos siglos se agazapan.[118]	centuries of meaning.

In "Danza, Mulata" (Dance, *Mulata*), he confesses:

Tú y yo sentimos en la sangre	You and I feel burning
galopar el incendio	in our veins
de una misma nostalgia...[119]	the fire of the same longing...

While the mulatto finds a certain spiritual re-creation in the movements of the dance, the poet recaptures lost ancestral meaning with his verses. In "La cumbia", which refers to an Afro-Colombian dance of the same name, Artel approaches a vision of the black woman as a symbol of the earth:

y la tierra,	and the earth
como una axila cálida de	like the warm armpit of a
negra.[120]	black woman.

In the works of the same poet are found variations on the treatment of the black woman as dancer. On the one hand, there is a description inspired by an obsession with her physical attributes and with the movement of her body as she dances the *rumba*, *cumbia*, or *merengue*; on the other hand, the poet may choose to delve beyond this superficial exterior and convey a profound image of her humanity.

The latter conversion, from an exotic, sensuous dancing figure to a cultural and humanistic symbol, is perhaps nowhere more sensitively manifested than in "Canción de la negra Juana" (Song of the Black Woman Juana) by the Venezuelan poet Miguel Rodríguez-Cárdenas (b. 1912). Juana, the product of the "dusty and run-down streets" of the *barrio* (neighborhood), gets ready to dance at the Carnival. Anticipating her participation, the whole neighborhood is astir with excitement and color. Juana is presented dressed for the occasion:

cintarajos de colores	on her head she wears
sobre la frente se ha puesto;	colored ribbons;
en el pecho una magnolia	on her breast, a magnolia,
y un malabar y un clavel.[121]	a malabar and a carnation.

As she winds her way to the Carnival site, neighborhood men greet her with praise for her beauty and charm. She responds with an invitation for all to join in the dancing.

...más que el palpitar	...more than the beat
de un ritmo	of a rhythm
parecen—muerta candela—	—a smouldering fire—
todo el ardor de una tribu	all the ardor of an
sedienta	eager tribe
sobre un tambor.[122]	on a drum.

When the dance ends, and the glitter has faded, the lonely Juana walks through the streets of her *barrio* remembering past hardships and the future, which promises monotony and loneliness:

en la vida sin amores	a life without love
que la espera, porque es negra	awaits her, because she is black
y las negras no conocen	and black women cannot hope for
ni novios ni matrimonios.[123]	sweethearts or marriage.

Three days later, Juana, the "black rose of the neighborhood" dies, leaving the neighbors to mourn for years to come. Here, Rodríguez-Cárdenas has created something loftier than just a black girl furiously dancing a *merengue* or a *joropo*:

porque Juanita es el alma-	because little Juana is the soul-
mater de mi barrio abstracto:	mother of my abstract ghetto:
síntesis de los abuelos	synthesis of all the ancestors
de toda la vecindad.[124]	of the neighborhood.

Notes

[1] Leslie Rout, Jr., *The African Experience in Latin America: 1502 to the Present Day* (London: Cambridge University Press, 1976), p. 14.
[2] Rout, pp. 15 and 16.
[3] Mónica Mansour, *La Poesía Negrista* (Mexico: Ediciones Era, 1973), p. 31.
[4] Miriam DeCosta, "The Portrayal of Blacks in a Spanish Medieval Manuscript," *Negro History Bulletin*, 37 (1974), 192.
[5] Mansour, p. 31.
[6] Margaret Sampson, "Africa in Medieval Spanish Literature: Its Appearance in *El Caballero Cifar*," *Negro History Bulletin*, 32 (1969), 15.
[7] Luis Monguío, "El negro en algunos poetas españoles y americanos anteriores a 1800," *Revista Iberoamericana*, 22 (1957), 248.
[8] Monguío, p. 249.
[9] Bruce Wardropper, "The Color Problem in Spanish Traditional Poetry," *MLN*, 75 (1960), 415.
[10] Wardropper, p. 415.
[11] José María Alín, *El cancionero español de tipo tradicional* (Madrid: Taurus, 1968), p. 254.
[12] Alín, p. 254.
[13] Alín, p. 516.
[14] Alín, p. 517.
[15] Alín, p. 517.
[16] Wardropper, p. 416
[17] Wardropper, p. 416.
[18] Alín, p. 254.
[19] Alín, p. 531.
[20] Alín, p. 632.
[21] Alín, p. 653.
[22] Alín, p. 570.
[23] Alín, p. 585.
[24] Alín, p. 257.
[25] Alín, p. 257.
[26] Alín, p. 257.
[27] Alín, p. 258.
[28] Moreno Villa as quoted in Fernando Ortiz and Rafael Marquina, "The Negro in the Spanish Theater," *Phylon*, 4 (1943), 150. Article trans-

slated by E. Irene Diggs.
[29] Ortiz and Marquina, p. 150.
[30] Velaurez B. Spratlin, "The Negro in Spanish Literature" in *Blacks in Hispanic Literature: Critical Essays*, editor, Miriam DeCosta (Port Washington, NY: Kennikat Press, 1977), p. 48.
[31] Mansour, p. 41.
[32] Edmund de Chasca, "The Phonology of the Speech of Negroes in Early Spanish Drama," *Hispanic Review*, 14 (1946), 323.
[33] Juan R. Castellano, "El negro esclavo en el entremés del Siglo de Oro," *Hispania*, 44 (1961), 58.
[34] Castellano, p. 61.
[35] Mansour, p. 36.
[36] Mansour, p. 36.
[37] Mansour, p. 36.
[38] Carter G. Woodson, "Attitudes of the Iberian Peninsula (in Literature)," in *Blacks in Hispanic Literature*, pp. 40-41. (Full citation: note 30)
[39] Ortiz and Marquina, p. 146.
[40] John Brooks, "Slavery in the Works of Lope de Vega," *Romanic Review*, 19 (1928), 239.
[41] Raymond S. Sayers, *The Negro in Brazilian Literature* (New York: Hispanic Institute in the United States, 1956), p. 27.
[42] Sayers, p. 27.
[43] Sayers, p. 27.
[44] Sayers, p. 25.
[45] Ortiz and Marquina, p. 146.
[46] Mansour, p. 34.
[47] Mansour, p. 34.
[48] Mansour, p. 34.
[49] Mansour, p. 38.
[50] Mansour, p. 38.
[51] Francisco de Quevedo, *Obras Completas, I*. 3rd ed. (Barcelona: Editorial Planeta, 1971), p. 819.
[52] Quevedo, p. 819.
[53] Quevedo, p. 819.
[54] Martha Cobb, "Afro-Arabs, Blackamoors, and Blacks: An Inquiry into Race Concepts Through Spanish Literature," *Black World*, 21, No. 4 (1972), 39.
[55] Miriam DeCosta, "The Evolution of the *Tema Negro* in the Literature of the Spanish Baroque," *CLA Journal*, 17 (1974), 420.
[56] Lemuel A. Johnson, *The Devil, the Gargoyle, and the Buffoon: The Negro as Metaphor in Western Literature* (Port Washington, N.Y.: Kennikat Press, 1969, 1971), p. 72.
[57] Rosa E. Valdés-Cruz, *La Poesia Negroide en América* (New York: Las Américas, 1970), p. 34.

[58] Sylvia Wynter, "The Eye of the Other: Images of the Black in Spanish Literature," in *Blacks in Hispanic Literature*, p. 17. (Full citation: note 30)
[59] Oscar Sambrano Urdaneta and Domingo Miliani, *Literatura Hispanoamericana: Manual/Antología*, Vol. I (Caracas: Editorial Texto, 1971), p. 92.
[60] Concha Meléndez, "Sor Juana y los negros," in *Signos de Iberoamérica* (Mexico: Manuel León Sánchez, S.C.L., 1936), pp. 85-86.
[61] Meléndez, pp. 85-86.
[62] Meléndez, pp. 85-86.
[63] Mansour, p. 61.
[64] Mansour, p. 62.
[65] Monguío, p. 257.
[66] Mansour, p. 60.
[67] Mansour, p. 70.
[68] Rout, p. 221.
[69] Monguío, p. 257.
[70] Mansour, pp. 63-64.
[71] José Juan Arrom, *Certidumbre de América* (Madrid: Gredos, 1971), p. 122.
[72] Arrom, p. 135.
[73] Arrom, p. 137.
[74] The folk poetry quoted in this section is all from José Juan Arrom, *Certidumbre de América* (Madrid: Gredos, 1971). Page numbers refer to this reference.
[75] Wilfred Cartey, *Black Images* (New York: Teachers College Press, 1970), p. 9.
[76] Cartey, pp. 9-10. Spanish text and translation.
[77] Hortensia Ruiz del Vizo, *Black Poetry of the Americas: A Bilingual Anthology* (Miami: Ediciones Universal, 1972), p. 91.
[78] Richard L. Jackson, *Black Writers in Latin America* (Albuquerque: University of New Mexico Press, 1979), pp. 53-54.
[79] Ann Venture Young, "The Black Woman in Afro-Caribbean Poetry," in *Blacks in Hispanic Literature*, p. 141. (Full citation: note 30)
[80] Enrique Noble, *Literatura Afro-Hispanoamericana* (Lexington, Massachusetts: Xerox College Publishing, 1973), p. 78.
[81] Mansour, p. 115. "En este poema el ambiente ha sido creado con palabras que insinúan ritmo, color, trópico, palabras sensuales, palabras para ser vistas, oídas, saboreadas, y sentidas."
[82] Noble, pp. 90-91.
[83] Noble, p. 85.
[84] Valdés-Cruz, p. 196.
[85] Mansour, p. 121.
[86] Valdés-Cruz, p. 197.
[87] Valdés-Cruz, p. 22. "Los poetas sienten verdadero deleite en detallar con gráficas expresiones el traje y el pañuelo de la bailadora, pero les

interesa mucho el cuerpo: sus ojos, los brazos, los dientes, los senos; pero, sobre todo, las caderas y las nalgas (grupas, ancas, flanco). La poesía blanca prefiere las curvas pectorales y el triángulo púbico, pero no hay poeta negroide que no se haya sentido incitado a usar metáforas gluteas..."

[88] Ruiz del Vizo, p. 39.
[89] Jorge Luis Morales, *Poesía Afroantillana y Negrista: Puerto Rico, República Dominicana, Cuba* (Rio Piedras: Editorial Universitaria, 1976), p. 223.
[90] Kay Boulware, "Woman and Nature in *Negrismo*," *Studies in Afro-Hispanic Literature*, I (1977), pp. 16-17.
[91] Boulware, pp. 16-17.
[92] Boulware, pp. 16-17.
[93] Boulware, pp. 16-17.
[94] Constance Sparrow de García-Barrio, "The Image of the Black Man in the Poetry of Nicolás Guillén," in *Blacks in Hispanic Literature*, p. 107. (Full citation: note 30)
[95] Morales, p. 193.
[96] Federico de Onís, "Introducción," in Luis Palés Matos, *Poesía (1915-1956)* (San Juan: Editorial Universidad de Puerto Rico, 1957), pp. 7-8.
[97] Luis Palés Matos, *Poesía (1915-1956)* (San Juan: Editorial Universidad de Puerto Rico, 1957), p. 219.
[98] G.R. Coulthard, *Race and Colour in Caribbean Literature* (London: Oxford University Press, 1962), pp. 89-90.
[99] Palés Matos, p. 245.
[100] The Caribbean poetry quoted in this section is all from Morales, *Poesía Afroantillana y Negrista*. Page numbers refer to this reference.
[101] Morales, p. 258.
[102] Andrea B. Rushing, "Images of Black Women in Modern African Poetry," in *Sturdy Black Bridges: Visions of Black Women in Literature* (New York: Anchor Books, 1979), p. 19.
[103] Nicomedes Santa Cruz, *Ritmos Negros del Perú* (Buenos Aires: Losada, 1971), pp. 95 and 96.
[104] Santa Cruz, pp. 95 and 96.
[105] Santa Cruz, p. 13.
[106] Pilar E. Barrios, *Piel Negra: Poesías (1917-1947)* (Montevideo: Nuestra Raza, 1947), p. 53.
[107] Miguel Otero Silva, *Poesía Completa* (Caracas: Monte Avila Editores, 1972), pp. 150-51.
[108] Otero Silva, pp. 150-51.
[109] Virginia Brindis de Salas, *Pregón de Marimorena* (Montevideo: Sociedad Cultural Editora Indoamericana, 1946), p. 37.
[110] Brindis de Salas, p. 35.
[111] Brindis de Salas, p. 38.
[112] Brindis de Salas, p. 34.

113 Helcías Martán Góngora, *Suma Poética (1963-1968)* (Ediciones de la Revista Ximénez de Quesada, 1969), p. 128.
114 Martán Góngora, pp. 144-45.
115 Noble, p. 68.
116 Ruiz del Vizo, p. 93.
117 Valdés-Cruz, p. 206.
118 Hortensia Ruiz del Vizo, *Poesía Negra del Caribe y Otras Areas* (Miami: Ediciones Universal, 1972), p. 127.
119 Ruiz del Vizo, p. 127.
120 Mansour, p. 205.
121 Miguel Rodríguez-Cárdenas, *Tambor: Poemas para Negros y Mulatos* (Caracas: Editorial "Elite", 1938), p. 22.
122 Rodríguez-Cárdenas, p. 22.
123 Rodríguez-Cárdenas, p. 22.
124 Rodríguez-Cárdenas, p. 22.

COLOMBIA

Candelario Obeso	"La Oberencia Filiá" "Canción del Boga Ausente"
Arturo Camacho Ramírez	"Bamba"
Hugo Salazar Valdés	"La Negra María Teresa" "Historia de Mary Bann" "Baile Negro"
Helcías Martán Góngora	"Hada Madrina" "Preludio Para Leonor González Mina" "Pejca" "Blasón" "Decir"
Juan Zapata Olivella	"Negrita Claridad" "La Mulata"
Jorge Artel	"Bullerengue" "Danza, Mulata" "La Cumbia"

Candelario Obeso

Candelario Obeso, poet and novelist, was born in the region of Mampos, Colombia, on January 12, 1849. Although lacking an early formal education, Obeso was well-versed in various academic disciplines, especially European literature. He also mastered several languages, including English, French, and Italian, for which he wrote language textbooks. Translations of Longfellow, Hugo, Musset, and Shakespeare comprise some of his published works.[1] His best known work is *Cantos populares de mi tierra* (Folk Songs of My Native Land), published in 1877, in which he faithfully captures the songs of the black *bateleros* (boatmen) of the Magdalena River by reproducing the distinctive characteristics of their speech.

Some literary critics consider Obeso the true forerunner of 20th-century black poetry in Latin America. Others have sought to diminish the importance of his contribution by labeling him a Romantic. In his lecture, "The Development of Black Literature in Hispanic America," the well-known Hispanist and historian Stanley A. Cyrus noted that Obeso was indeed a Romantic but that his poetry, written more than 100 years ago, already contained many of the elements of black poetry as we know it today. Cyrus cited the much-anthologized poem, "Canción de la boga ausente" (Song of the Lonely Oarsman), as an example of the musicality Obeso achieves.[2] This musicality became a dominant element of black poetry of the 20th century.

Another dimension common to both the poetry of Obeso and subsequent black poetry is the element of social protest. The celebrated Cuban poet Nicolás Guillén comments on its presence in Obeso's work when he explains that the Colombian poet

> was not only a creative artist who wrote in the manner of the black Colombian who heavily populates the Magdalena region .... He captured their peculiar rhythm, that of the *cumbia*, which bears resemblance to our *son*. But sometimes he went even further, and left poems that carry a revolutionary sense, which, if not manifest in a violent and vindictive manner, is emitted through his expression of the hidden grief the common man suffers in the face of social injustice ...[3]

In the poems of the 19th-century Obeso, we find a clear expression of black identity and pride; a testimony to the harsh realities characteristic of the lives of black folk in his native land; an undeniable protest against those bitter realities of the black experience; and the presentation of authentic black speech. Richard L. Jackson is quite right when he places Obeso in the vanguard of the development of poetry with a genuine and unique black sensibility which shows a devotion to black culture, black people, and black themes.[4]

I include two examples of Candelario Obeso's poetry in this anthology of 20th-century black poetry because, like Jackson, I am convinced that this black Colombian poet deserves to be recognized as a genuine precursor of the black poetry which followed.

LA OBERIENCIA FILIÁ

Candelario Obeso

—Me ha richo uté que juiga re los hombre,
    y yo les he juío;
sólo, a la vece cuando er só se junde
convécso con Rogelio en er camino...

—¿Si?...¿qué te rice?...—Que me quiere mucho...
    Yo naitica le rigo;
—¿Y luego?...—Añare un apretón re mano,
o me ra en er cachete argún besito...

—Ejtá güeno...¡junju!...¿Conque tó eso
    te jace ese lambio?
A pajareá no güerva j'a la roza,
pocque tás, mi hija e mi arma, en un peligro...

—¡Fue ansina siempre er hombre!...Re panela
    se juntan er jocico,
y a la pendeja como tú la engañan
pa yevála mansita ar precepicio...

—Mama...¡varay!...no embrome...¡Ese muchacho
    tiene su labio limpio!...
Y si viene en mi junta, me arza en peso,
cuando muy barrialoso tá er camino...

—Eja son suj artimaña...Re muchacha
    me sucerió lo mimo...
Echa a tu fló, mi hijita, cuatro ñuro,
y no orvire jamá lo que te he richo...

                 * * *

FILIAL OBEDIENCE

Candelario Obeso

—You told me to stay away from men,
   And I have done that;
except when the sun goes down
I talk to Rogelio on the road...

—Oh?... And what does he say?... —That he loves me...
   But I don't say anything;
—And then?... —He holds my hand a little,
or gives me a little kiss on the cheek...

—Ah ha!... I see... So that's all
   the rascal does to you?
Don't hang around that place anymore,
because you're in danger, my child...

—Men have always been that way!... They speak
   sweet nothings,
and they deceive naive girls like you
leading them off meekly to ruin.

—Mama... For goodness sake! Don't worry... That boy
   speaks sincerely!...
And if he comes to meet me, he lifts me up bodily
when the road is muddy.

—That's a part of his scheme... As a girl
   the same thing happened to me...
Tie four knots in your flower, my child,
and never forget what I have told you...

* * *

Ar otro día muy poc la mañana
    gizo la chica un lio...
Er só muy lejo la topó sin flore
entre lo tierno brazo der peligro...
En ninguna ocasión consejo e viejas
    má que en ejta han servio...
¡Cuando pica er amó lo pecho joven
se acaba la oberencia re los hijo!...

The next day, early in the morning
    the girl got caught...
The sun found her far away, without flowers,
in the tender arms of danger...
Never has the advice of old women
served any better than in this case...
When love strikes the youthful breast,
filial obedience ends.

CANCIÓN DEL BOGA AUSENTE

Candelario Obeso

    Qué trijte que etá la noche,
      La noche que trijte etá;
No hay en er cielo una estrella
      Remá, remá.

    La negra re mi arma mía,
      Mientras yo brego en la ma,
Bañao en suró por ella,
      ¿Qué hará? ¿Qué hará?

    Tar ve por su zambo amao
      Doriente sujpirará,
O tar ve ni recuerda...
      ¡Llorá! ¡Llorá!

    Las jembras son como toro
      lo rojta tierra ejgraciá;
Con acte se saca er peje
      ¡Der má, der má!

    Con acte se abranda er jiero,
      Se roma la mapaná...
Cojtante y ficme la penaj;
      ¡No hay ma, no hay ma!

    Qué ejcura que etá la noche,
      la noche que ejcura etá;
Asina ejcura e la ausencia
      ¡Bogá, bogá!

SONG OF THE LONELY OARSMAN

Candelario Obeso

> How sad is the night,
>   the night, how sad it is.
> In the sky, not a single star.
>   Row on, row on!
>
> The black woman of my soul,
>   While I'm struggling at sea,
> bathed in sweat for her,
>   what's she up to?
>
> Maybe for her beloved "zambo"[5]
>   she's sighing with grief,
> or maybe she don't remember me...
>   Cry on, cry on!
>
> Women are like bulls,
>   a misfortune in this land.
> With skill you catch the fish
>   from the sea, from the sea...
>
> With skill you soften iron,
>   tame the poisonous snake...
> The pain is sharp and steady.
>   There's nothing left!
>
> How dark is the night,
>   the night, how dark it is;
> loneliness is also dark.
>   Row on, row on!

Arturo Camacho Ramírez

Arturo Camacho Ramírez, born in Colombia in 1909, is considered a member of the group of Colombian poets involved in *Piedra y Cielo* (Stone and Sky), a short-lived literary movement that reached its apogee around 1940. The critic Eduardo Gómez, who wrote the prologue to Camacho's volume of poems *Carrera de la vida* (The Course of Life), tentatively dates the beginning of the movement with the publication of the first poems of Camacho Ramírez in 1935.

The *Piedra y Cielo* poets affirmed the importance and influence of the 20th-century Peninsular Spanish poets, especially Juan Ramón Jiménez and various members of the group known as the "Generation of '27": Luis Cernuda, Federico García Lorca, Rafael Alberti, Vicente Aleixandre, and Jorge Guillén. The Colombian poets were also inspired by the Latin American poets Vicente Huidobro and Pablo Neruda.[6] The *piedracielistas*, who took their name from Jiménez' work published in 1919, rejected what they considered excessive traditionalism in Colombian poetry.[7]

Camacho Ramírez' books of poetry include *Espejo de naufragio* (Reflections on a Shipwreck), 1935; *Presagio de amor* (A Token of Love), 1939; *Oda a Carlos Baudelaire* (Ode to Charles Baudelaire), 1945; *La vida pública* (Public Life), 1962; *Límites del hombre* (The Limits of Man), 1964; and *Carrera de la vida* (The Course of Life), 1976. In addition to his active literary life, Camacho did a stint as the Colombian representative to the United Nations Educational, Scientific, and Cultural Organization (UNESCO) in Bolivia.

Camacho Ramírez' art, like that of his fellow *piedracielistas*, seeks to achieve a balance between incursions into the world of imagination and fantasy, symbolized by the sky (*el cielo*) and the representation of the often harsh American realities, symbolized by the stone (*la piedra*). The poem "Bamba" which follows, in which the poet resorts to portraying a fairly typical figure of the black woman as a sensually frenetic rumba dancer, derives from the *piedra* inspiration.

BAMBA

Arturo Camacho Ramírez

¡Bamba, Bamba, Bamba,
qué palo de negra, zamba
candonga!

Tu boca bemba y rezonga
sílaba negra que zumba.

Aoeeech... aaaah...
comba la cintura ya,
combaláaa...

Bamba, como una llama que arde en la madrugada
asida al leño ardiente de su lujuria fresca,
se desgaja en racimos de eternidad que crujen
sobre su dorso húmedo, sobre su danza crespa.

Bamba retumba y tiembla rodando por la rambla
con sus rampantes crines de resonante tromba.
Bamba, atada a la noche, se tumba entre la sombra
mordida por los sobrios tambores de la rumba.

¡Bamba, Bamba, Bamba,
qué palo de negra, zamba
candonga!

Bamba se bambolea como bullente bomba,
burbuja que brota su burbullante cimba.
Quimba zamba del negro brincando por la chamba,
de las piernas que ofrecen su rechinante timba.
Bamba negra: en el ritmo de tu carne deshilada
retuerce en torbellinos tu piel lechosa y turbia;
esparce sus caderas con frenesí sonámbulo.
flotando entre tambores de miel picante y rubia.

BAMBA

Arturo Camacho Ramírez

Bamba, Bamba, Bamba,
what a fine black girl, zamba[5]
candonga!

Your thick lips mutter
black sounds which buzz.

Aoeech... aaaah...
Let me see you shake yourself,
shake, girl, shake.

Bamba, like a flame that burns in the dawn
clinging to the burning log of its fresh desire,
shatters into particles of eternity that crackle
on her humid back, on her brisk dancing.

Bamba shakes and trembles spinning on the ground
with her wild mane resounding.
Bamba, chained to the darkness, tumbles in the shadow
seized by the somber drums of the rumba.

Bamba, Bamba, Bamba,
what a fine black girl, zamba
candonga!

Bamba moves herself like a sizzling bomb, noise giving birth to more noise.
Black sandal of the negro jumping on the field,
of the legs which offer his trembling belly.
Black Bamba: to the beat of your deceitful flesh
your ripe and turbulent body whirls;
she shakes her hips with somnambulant frenzy,
floating among drums of pungent and golden honey.

¡Bamba, Bamba, Bamba,
qué palo de negra, zamba
candonga!

Bamba, Bamba, Bamba,
what a fine black girl, zamba
candonga!

Hugo Salazar Valdés

Hugo Salazar Valdés (b. 1924) is a native a Chocó, Colombia, an area inhabited predominantly by blacks. "He was a literature professor, but above all a lover of adventure, one who hitchhiked around various countries, sleeping in parks, and reciting his poetry to earn money on which to live. In 1971, he is credited with having boasted that he had earned a livelihood for five years by reciting poetry, without ever including in his recitals poems by poets other than himself."[8] After these years as an itinerant poet, Salazar came to Bogotá, where he served as the Director of Popular Culture.

As a native of the Chocó, Salazar's observations of black Colombian culture are first-hand. Colombian critic Jaime Mejia Duque considers Hugo Salazar Valdés to be the chief representative of the poetry of the Chocó region.[9] Some examples of this poetry are contained in his volume *Dimensión de la tierra* (Dimensions of the Earth), 1952. Other published works of poetry include *Mar inicial* (The First Sea); *Carbones en el alba* (Coals in the Dawn), 1948; *Las raices sonoras* (The Sonorous Roota), 1976; *Casi la luz* (Almost Light), 1954; *La patria convocada* (Fatherland Summoned), 1955; *El héroe cantado* (The Praised Hero), 1956; and *Toda la voz* (The Whole Voice), 1960.

Of Salazar's poems on the black theme, Hortensia Ruiz del Vizo maintains that "they have won him an undisputable place in the Colombian Parnassus. His (the poet's) obsession with black dances has led him to devote several compositions to this element in the black culture. Salazar Valdés has succeeded in incarnating the vividness and musicality of these dances. Although he rather clings to traditional modes of depiction, he has nevertheless managed to infuse into these creations an *élan vital*."[10]

In his poems presented in this anthology, Salazar Valdés offers portraits of three black women, all admirable dancers of the African-inspired rumba or *cumbia*. In "La negra María Teresa," the poet emphasizes, in somewhat burlesque fashion, the blackness of María Teresa's skin and eyes:

Oscura, de tinta china,	Dark like India ink,
pupilas de lumbre mora,	eyes of blackberry light,
piel de betún y de brea,	skin of boot-black and tar
y las manos como dos	and hands like two black
guillotinadoras negras.	guillotines.

His *cumbia* dancer is described as:

    casi loca, casi eléctrica,   almost frenzied, almost electric
    casi infantil, casi bárbara...   almost childish, almost savage...

  Amid the sounds of the drum, the bongo, the flute, the maracas, and the cymbals, the black rumba dancer of "Baile negro" "danza mil maravillas/en la lucha de la rumba" (dances marvelously in the battle of the rumba). She is joined in her wild dance by the *negro*, "rítmico, loco,/carbón de ébano, betún..." (rhythmic, wild/ebony charcoal,/tar...) In the poem Salazar expresses his disgust with his people who, in their abandon, seek to recapture the by-gone visions of Africa. The poem ends by praising the dancing prowess of the dancers but regretting their drunken abandon.

  In "Historia de Mary Bann", Salazar Valdés departs from the candid sensuality of "La negra María Teresa" and "Baile negro". Whereas in those two poems the reader is bombarded with loud music, frenzied dancing, and drunkenness, here, although the same elements—the musical instruments, the rum, the rumba—are present, everything is muted and refined. It compels with its delicacy of expression.

LA NEGRA MARÍA TERESA

Hugo Salazar Valdés

Oscura, de tinta china,
era la María Teresa:
pupilas de lumbre mora,
piel de betún y de brea,
sonrisa de caña dulce
su boca de miel de abejas
y las manos como dos
guillotinadoras negras.

Nunca supieron mis ojos
ola de mar más violenta:
danzando la cumbia solo
se puede pensar en ella,
en el trópico vehemente
y oblicuo de sus caderas
como una llama creciendo
en el volcán de las piernas.

El alcohol del currulao
la hundía entre las tinieblas;
bajo el vestido, los senos
tombaban voz de protesta,
en actitud de luceros
varoniles, por la tierra,
y eran como dos palomas
esquivas que no se acercan.

María Teresa jugaba
las manos como culebras,
en marejadas de ritmo,
casi loca, casi eléctrica,
casi infantil, casi bárbara,
entre azogues que envenenan,
y era una noche con luna
la sonrisa de la negra.

THE BLACK GIRL MARIA TERESA

Hugo Salazar Valdés

Dark, like India ink
was María Teresa:
eyes of blackberry light,
skin of boot-black and tar,
smile of sweet sugar cane
her mouth of bee's honey
and hands like two
black guillotines.

My eyes have never seen
an ocean wave more violent:
dancing the "cumbia", one
can only think of her,
of the vehement and oblique
curve of her hips
like a swelling flame
in the volcano of her legs.

The potency of the rum
drowned her in the darkness;
beneath her dress, her breasts
raised a voice of protest,
like spirited morning stars,
throughout the land,
and they were as two elusive
doves keeping their distance.

Maria Teresa moved
her hands like a snake,
in rhythmic excitement,
almost frenzied, almost electric,
almost childish, almost savage,
amidst quicksilver that poisons,
and the smile of the "negra"
was like a moonlit night.

Prendida de ron podia
verse el fuego de la herencia:
negra, de africana estirpe,
por la sala cumbiambera,
dengueándose de lujuria,
ya de ron, ya de candela,
ya de aguardiente o guarapo,
repicando con las piernas,
iba enseñando las fauces
de sus enaguas tremendas.

El "bon bon" de la tambora,
el "chingui chingui" que enerva,
el "firilú firilú"
de la flauta nocherniega
y el "tren tren" de la requinta
pólvora de la demencia,
sabian que era un ¡arriba!
de corazón y de arengas.

"Ay, ay, que me tá quemando
la sangre entre laj acterias;
Vigen rel Cajmen, Maria,
San Antonio, Santa Elena,
la calentura mi gente,
la juelza je la arrechera
y er picaro rel injuante
¡que me tiene toa ejtrecha!"

Con este decir atávico,
turbio como su presencia,
entre la hoguera del baile,
mordida por mil flaquezas,
con los brazos entreabiertos
y las manos con dos velas,
se recreaba en la sala
¡la negra María Teresa!

Drunk with rum
the fire of her ancestors reared
black girl, of African heritage,
in the throes of the dance,
her body twisting with desire,
then with rum, then with fire,
with "aguardiente", or guarapo[11]
moving her legs furiously,
showing the hems
of her enormous petticoats.

The *bon bon* of the drummer,
the *chingui chingui* which enervates,
the *firilu firilu*
of the night-wandering flute
and the *tren tren* of the wanton
vivacity of folly,
they knew that it was a shout
from her heart and soul.

"Ay, ay, the blood in my veins
is burning me up;
Oh Virgin Carmen, Mary
Saint Anthony, Saint Helen,
the fever of my people,
the frenzy of the wild one
and that devil of a rogue
that have me all confused!"

With that atavistic speech,
as disturbing as her manner,
in the heat of the dance,
seized by a thousand weaknesses,
with her arms half-opened
a candle in each hand,
she came alive in the room
the black girl, Maria Teresa.

HISTORIA DE MARY BANN

Hugo Salazar Valdés

Fue en un amanecer de libaciones
con marineros y guitarras,
marimbas y tambores.

Era una moza de candela y rosa
que danzaba la danza de los cuentos,
Mary Bann se llamaba.
La rumba se sumaba al embrujo
de sus caderas fértiles, de ébano,
que en bárbaras cadencias
prendía hogueras de sol en el cerebro.

La llama de su boca
despertaba la fiebre de los besos
y encendido deseo de naufragio
la marea bicorne de su pecho.

En la piratería de sus brazos
el ritmo era el aforno de embelesos,
bajo la cabellera desflecada,
en los hombros eléctricos,
que hacía pensar en la princesa ebria
de algún imperio negro.
Su cuerpo de ciclón desenfrenado
retaba lo epiléptico.

Como un audaz grumete de oleajes
en la febril ribera de sus brazos
anclé la ansiosa proa de mi nave,
y en espiral de buzo loco,
la tropical herencia de mi sangre
descendió a sus abismos
y acalló los impulsos ancestrales.

THE STORY OF MARY BANN

Hugo Salazar Valdés

It was a late night of revelry
with sailors and guitars,
marimbas and drums.

She was a girl of fire and rose
who danced the dance of the folktales;
her name was Mary Bann.
The rumba succumbed to the magic
of her fertile hips, of ebony,
which in barbarous cadences
dazzled the onlooker.

The flame of her mouth
awoke the fever of her kisses
and the lively desire to be shipwrecked
on the bicorn tide of her chest.

In the piracy of her arms
rhythm was the ecstatic garnish,
beneath her wooly hair,
around her electric shoulders,
reminiscent of an intoxicated princess
of some black empire.
Her body like a convulsive cyclone
challenged epileptic frenzy.

Like a daring surge of waves
in the feverish shore of her arms
I anchored the eager prow of my ship,
and in the plunge of a crazy diver,
the tropical inheritance of my blood
descended to its depths
and quieted the ancestral yearnings.

Fue en un amanecer de libaciones
con marineros y guitarras,
marimbas y tambores.

It was a late night of revelry
with sailors and guitars,
marimbas and drums.

BAILE NEGRO

Hugo Salazar Valdès

Tin tan, tin tan, tin tan,
suena el timbal;
porongo, bolongo, marongo,
suena el bongó;
gime la flauta,
ruge el tambor,
y entre los "chaquis" de la maraca
va el lagrimón.
¡La voz gitana de la marimba!
¡La sed doliente de las orillas!
La negra danza mil maravillas,
y entre su boca de rojo y negro
rieles, panderos y cascabeles y lunas brillan
Ay, ay, aiiiiiiii;
la negra da media vuelta,
sube los brazos,
y en la epilepsia de las caderas
hay fogonazos y batatazos,
y entre los senos, boas perversas,
como en los ojos de borrachera
laten los perros
de los ancestros
y de los ritos de África negra.
Chin, chin, chin,
son los platillos con voz de anis.
La negra danza mil maravillas
y es todo ritmo su desacuerdo;
luego se abaja, tiembla,
camina la vorágine del cuerpo;
y entre zalemas y giros,
salaz y ansioso,
por la escotilla,
la sigue el negro,
rítmico, loco,

BLACK DANCE

Hugo Salazar Valdés

Tin tan, tin tan, tin tan,
sounds the drum;
porongo, bolongo, marongo,
beats the bongo;
the flute groans,
the drum roars,
and amid the *chaquis* of the maraca
the guitar is heard.
The gypsy voice of the marimba!
The dolorous tone of the drum!
The black girl dances marvelously,
and in her mouth of red and black
rings and tambourines, bells and moons shine
Ay, ay, aiiiiiiii;
the *Negra* makes a half turn,
raises her arms,
and in the epilepsy of her hips
there are convulsions and seizures,
and in her breasts, perverse boas,
as in her two drunken eyes,
the dogs
of the ancestors
and of black African rituals howl.
Chin, chin, chin
sound the cymbals with licorice voice.
The *Negra* dances marvelously
and her discord is all rhythm;
then she bends, trembles,
and twirls her body;
and with bows and turns,
salacious and eager,
the *Negro* follows her,
on the journey,
rhythmic, wild,

carbón de ébano,
betún, vigilia,
noche de vida,
grito sus miembros...
Sudan petróleo los negros
en la lucha de la rumba;
el hierro de la alegría
sobre el yunque de la angustia
galopa la voz alcohólica
de las visiones esdrújulas;
rompe el cielo de los cocos
las estridencias agudas,
el negro sigue danzando
tras de la fugaz cintura,
y hay un instante en que el cuerpo
parece de caucho y música.
Chin, chin, chin,
son los platillos con voz de anís;
porongo, bolongo, marongo,
suena el bongó;
gime la flauta,
ruge el tambor,
y entre los "chasquis" de la maraca
va el lagrimón...
Los negros danzan mil maravillas,
los negros matan sus agonías,
los negros beben y se emborrachan;
¡ah, raza mía!

ebony charcoal,
tar, vigil
life-giving night,
pure sound his body...
Negros sweat petroleum
in the battle of the rumba;
the iron of joy
over the anvil of anxiety,
the drunken voice
of by-gone visions gallops;
the heaven of the tropics breaks
the sharp stridences,
the black man keeps on dancing
behind the fleeing waist,
for a moment his body
seems made of rubber and music.
Chin, chin, chin,
sound the cymbals with licorice voice;
porongo, bolongo, marongo,
beats the bongo;
the flute groans,
the drum roars,
and amid the *chaquis* of the maraca
the guitar is heard.
The blacks dance marvelously,
the blacks forget their agonies,
the blacks drink and get drunk;
ah, my people!

Helcías Martán Góngora

Helcías Martán Góngora was born around 1920 in the department of Cauca, Colombia. The western portion of Cauca forms a part of the Pacific coast lowlands where a large proportion of the inhabitants are of African descent. The Pacific Ocean and its coastal regions are frequent motifs in the poetry of Martán Góngora.[12]

The poet holds the doctor of law degree from the University of Bogota. He served as the Secretary of Education in Cauca, director of the Escuela Nacional de Folclor (National School of Folklore), and director of the Teatro Colón (Colon Theater). Martán Góngora directed the cultural journals of the Universidad Nacional and the Universidad de Cauca and wrote for a number of Colombian newspapers and journals.[13]

His published collections of poetry include *Océano* (Ocean), *Canciones y jardines* (Songs and Gardens), *Lejana patria* (Distant Fatherland), *Nuevo laberinto* (New Labyrinth), *Memoria de la infancia* (Childhood Memory), *Encadenado a las palabras* (Prisoner of Words), 1963; *La rosa de papel* (Paper Rose), *Los pasos en la sombra* (Footsteps in the Shadows), 1964; *Casa de caracol* (House of Snails), 1965; *Treno* (Lament), 1966; and *Diario del crepúsculo* (Twilight Diary).

In 1969 Martán Góngora published his *Suma poética*, poetry written between 1963 and 1969. Much of his poetry on the black theme was composed during this period and is contained in this volume. Among these poems from *Suma poética* are four of the compositions which follow: "Preludio para Leonor González Mina" (Prelude for Leonor González Mina), "Fabla negra" (Black Tale), "Blasón" (Family Emblem), and "Decir" (A Saying).

In his treatment of black women, Martán Góngora departs from the stereotypical portrayals characteristic of some of the earlier poets of the genre, who emphasize sensuality and sexuality.[14] Typical of Martán Góngora's black women is the Colombian singer of popular folk songs, Leonor González Mina, whom he praises for her physical and spiritual beauty.

HADA MADRINA

A Eufemia Meza

Helcías Martán Góngora

Morena
vara
de azucena.
Fue casta, dulce y buena
Fue como el agua clara
de una fuente serena,
sin sombra de pecado,
sin huellas en la arena.
Su muerte es viva espina
hundida en mi costado.
A toda golondrina
y al viento le he confiado
su ramo de fragancia...
¡Si fue el hada madrina
del cuento de mi infancia!

FAIRY GODMOTHER

For Eufemia Meza

Helcías Martán Góngora

>   Brown
>   stem
>   of the lily.
>   She was chaste, sweet and good.
>   She was like the clear water
>   of a serene fountain,
>   without shadow of sin,
>   without footprints in the sand.
>   Her death is a vivid thorn
>   buried in my side.
>   To every swallow
>   and to the wind I have entrusted
>   her fragrant bouquet
>   She was the fairy godmother
>   of my childhood story!

PRELUDIO PARA LEONOR GONZÁLEZ MINA

Helcías Martán Góngora

Si digo que tu voz es una mina
de plata y esmeraldas, yo me entrego
a un melódico juego
de palabras, ¡Leonor González Mina!
Alondra negra, peregrina
vestal de oscura porcelana
que el amor ilumina
con su llama africana
y el ancestro conmina
a oficiar la liturgia americana
en la meseta andina.
Tañe tu cuerpo de arpa de obsidiana
el viento, con sus manos de palmera,
y el cantar es profética proclama
del negro que aún espera.
La sombra en ti se ufana
y traza una melódica frontera
en tu remota aldea,
al sur de una campana.
Tallada fuiste en la fluvial madera
en que se labra el lecho y la canoa.
Erguida estás en la sonora proa,
isla para el rumor de la marea,
icono de carbón, diosa de brea.
Sea por ti mi loa,
en la sombra estelar,
tu preludio, ¡Leonor!
sobre el tambor
del mar.

PRELUDE FOR LEONOR GONZÁLEZ MINA

Helcías Martán Góngora

If I say that your voice is a mine
of silver and emeralds, I am guilty
of a melodic play
on words, Leonor González Mina!,
Black lark, vestal
pilgrim of dark porcelain
which love illumines
with its African flames
and the ancestor threatens
to offer the American liturgy
on the Andean plateau.
The wind with its hands of palm
strums on your body like an obsidian harp,
and its singing is a prophetic proclamation
of the black man who still waits.
Darkness takes pride in you
and designs a melodic boundary
in your remote hamlet
to the south of the church bell.
You were sculpted from the fluvial wood
from which cradles and canoes are made.
You stand erect in the sonorous proa,
an island for the murmur of the tide,
charcoal icon, pitch black goddess.
May my praise for you be,
in the stellar shadow,
your prelude, Leonor!
on the drum
of the sea.

FABLA NEGRA

(A Hugo Cuevas Martán)

PEJCA

Helcías Martán Góngora

Voy a pejcate la luna
pa que voj pintéj la cuna
der hijo que me daráj.
Que no lo sepa tu mama,
ni tu prima, ni tu heimana,
ni er zambo de tu papá.

Voy a pejcate un lucero
pa iluminate er sendero
y ar niño que ha de llegá.
Dejá abierta la ventana
pa que te alumbre la cama
cuando voj solita ejtáj.

Er día que nazca mijo
pa mojtrate er regocijo
er mar te voy a pejcá,
así manque te muy lejo
er sor en cada reflejo
mi amor te recordará.

No creigaj que yo ejtoy loco
ni que dijvarío un poco.
Lo que te digo ej verdá.
Voy a pejcate una ejtrella
pa que voj juguéj con ella
y matéj la escurida.

BLACK TALE

(To Hugo Cuevas Martán)

FISHIN'

Helcías Martán Góngora

    I'm gonna catch you the moon
    so you can paint the cradle
    of the son you're gonna give me.
    Don't tell your momma,
    or your cousin, or your sister,
    or that *zambo*, your papa.[5]

    I'm gonna catch you a morning star,
    to light up the way for you
    and the kid who's on the way.
    Leave the window open,
    so that it can light up your bed
    when you're all by yourself.

    The day my son is born,
    to show you my delight
    I'm gonna catch you the sea,
    so even when I'm far away
    each reflection of the sun
    will remind you of my love.

    Don't think I'm crazy
    and that I'm off my rocker.
    What I'm telling you is true.
    I'm gonna catch you a star
    for you to play with
    and kill the darkness.

No hace juarta la atarraya
que puse a secá en la playa,
a la sombra der parmá,
poique a jembra que quiera
le pejco una tintorera
con una mano, ¡no má!

Er mar ej mi viejo amigo
y cuando sueño contigo
se amansa y pone a cantá.
Er mar sabe que en la proa
sin nombre de mi canoa
tu nombre voy a pintá.

Er mar sabe que no miento.
Lo sabe también er viento
que er cielo te voy a da
pa mojtrate er regocijo
er día que najca er hijo
que Dioj noj va a regalá.

I don't need that old casting net
that I left to dry on the sand,
in the shade of a palm tree,
'cause for the woman I love
I'll catch her a shark
with my one bare hand.

The sea is my old friend
and when I dream about you
it gets real tame and begins to sing.
The sea knows that on the nameless
prow of my canoe I'm gonna paint your name.

The sea knows I'm not lying.
The wind knows it too,
that I'm gonna give you the sky
to show you my joy
on the day the son is born
that God's gonna give us.

BLASÓN

Helcías Martán Góngora

Cuando enciende su congola
la señora bisabuela,
que presume de española,
al fulgor de la candela
—en que el tabaco se inmola—
es una sombra que vela
igual que el ánima-sola.

Carga y carga su congola
la señora bisabuela
con buen tabaco de bola
mientras alguien, en la escuela,
pisa al biznieto la cola
cuando orgulloso revela
que tiene sangre española.

Fuma y fuma su congola
y escucha latir la vela
de esclava nave española
y el humo—que lento vuela—
pone una blanca aureola
a la negra bisabuela.

En la funeraria estela
—en vez de extraña corola—
sea la humilde congola
blasón de la bisabuela.

FAMILY EMBLEM

Helcías Martán Góngora

When the great-grandmother,
who boasts of her Spanish blood,
lights up her cigar
from the flame of the fire
—in which the tobacco is cured—
she is a shadow which watches
like the lone spirit.

The great-grandmother
puffs and puffs on her cigar
made with a good tobacco
while at the school house,
they step on her grandson's tail
when he proudly announces
his Spanish heritage.

She smokes away on her cigar
and hears the flapping of the sails
of the Spanish slave boat
and the smoke—which slowly soars—
forms a white halo
around the black grandmother.

On her tombstone
—instead of an expensive cigar—
let the humble *congola* be
the grandmother's emblem.

DECIR

Helcias Martán Góngora

    Quiere ser blanca la moza
    que tiene la piel oscura.
    La luz del alba se goza
    en la nocturna estatura
    de la moza más garbosa
    que nació en Buenaventura!

    Rubia quiere ser la moza
    de piel color de tabaco.
    La luz de la mar se goza
    en la moza más garbosa
    que vio la luz en Tumaco!

A SAYING

Helcías Martán Góngora

> The girl with the dark skin
> wants to be white.
> The light of dawn frolics
> on the nocturnal figure
> of the loveliest girl
> ever born in Buenaventura.
>
> The tobacco-colored girl
> wants to be white.
> The light of the sea dances
> on the loveliest girl
> ever born in Tumaco.

Juan Zapata Olivella

Juan Zapata Olivella, poet and playwright, was born in Colombia around 1920. The name *Zapata* is well-known in the literary circles of Colombia. Manuel Zapata Olivella, his brother, is a noted Afro-Colombian novelist who lectured on the Colombian novel at Howard University (Washington, D.C.) and at other colleges and universities in North America. Manuel also numbers among the founders of the Instituto de Estudios Afrocolombianos (Institute of Afro-Colombian Studies), which hosted the 1977 conference of scholars of the African Diaspora, in Bogota and Cali.

Juan Zapata is the author of three volumes of poetry: *Gaitas bajo del sol* (Flutes Under the Sun), 1968; *Campanario incesante* (Eternal Tower), 1969; and *Albedrio total* (Free Will), 1970. His plays include the historical drama "El grito de Cartagena" (The Battle Cry of Cartagena), 1961 and the comedy "La Patoja," 1968.

According to Hortensia Ruiz del Vizo, Juan Zapata Olivella "belongs to the new generation of Colombian poets who have kept a faithful alliance to the black theme despite the fact that it (the black theme) does not constitute the heart of their poetry. In fact, Zapata is known as the 'poeta del amor' ('poet of love')."[15]

Zapata offers two distinct portrayals of black women in *Albedrio total*. In "Mulata", he depicts a new woman—a synthesis produced by the confluence of all the peoples of the world. This mulatto woman delights the poet with her firm silhouette, fine intelligence, and gentle look. Zapata contemplates the future with considerable optimism based on his apparent confidence in the powers and positive attributes of the mulatto woman.

By contrast, the tone of the poem "Negrita Claridad" is less sober and less philosophical. Here the poet describes every feature of her physical and sensual being: feet, teeth, belly, underarms, and breasts. Swaying to the happy rhythms, she is dance in its purest expression.

NEGRITA CLARIDAD

Juan Zapata Olivella

Mirá, que linda está
la negrita Claridá.
La piel oscura
y el nombre claro.

Mueve la cadera con agilidá,
menea los ojos en la oscuridá,
el son montuno,
el son mapalé,
el son más alegre,
el son de verdá,
es la danza negra
que con tó elají
sacude ese cuerpo
de azabache tibio
de tostao maní.

Muévete así, Claridá,
pies de tenaza,
sexo de alquitrán,
dientes de algodón,
barriga de tambó,
senos de huracán,
axila de trópico,
cintura de bambú,
manos de fogón,
labios de caimito,
fuerza de Sansón.

Candela, Candela,
ritmo de alegría.
Claridá que alumbra
de noche y de día.

THE BLACK GIRL CLARIDAD

Juan Zapata Olivella

    See how pretty,
    the black girl Claridá.
    Dark skin
    and bright name.

    She moves her hips with agility,
    moves her eyes in the darkness,
    the rustic sound,
    the *mapale* sound,
    the happiest sound,
    the sound of truth,
    the black rhythm
    which lovingly
    shakes that body
    of warm jet,
    of toasted nuts.

    Shake yourself, Claridá,
    feet like tongs,
    sex of tar,
    teeth like cotton,
    belly like a drum,
    hurricane breasts,
    tropical armpit,
    bamboo waist,
    hot hands,
    star apple lips,
    strength like Samson.

    Fire, Fire,
    rhythm of happiness.
    Claridá who brightens
    both night and day.

Baila otra vez, Claridá,
moja tus axilas
en la tinta negra
de tu mocedá.

Eres más linda,
eres el carbón,
eres pura danza,
pura sensación.

Si no fueras negra,
negra de verdá,
no te llamarían
negra Claridá.

Dance again, Claridá,
Dampen your armpits
in the black essence
of your youth.

You are the prettiest,
you are pure charcoal,
you are pure rhythm,
pure fascination.

If you weren't black,
truly black,
they wouldn't call you
the black girl Claridá.

LA MULATA

Juan Zapata Olivella

Si una sola raza dominara
no serian tus ojos, negros ojos,
tu pelo, espeso pelo,
y esa escama de tu piel
no tan bronceada.
Si los genes que te concibieron
fueran genes de una misma raza,
tu cuerpo tan esbelto de palmera
no daría ese tu talle de palmera.

Toda la hibridez de tu boca
es fruta sensual de todo trópico,
hay achiote en tus labios de Guinea
y esa audaz malicia en tu mirada
denuncia el temple del ancestro indígena.
Si miramos el mapa de tu cuerpo desnudo,
se asomarían todos los pueblos del mundo,
apurar un cocktail seria una dicha
servido en tus senos de ánforas de Grecia.

Qué silueta maciza,
que fina inteligencia,
y qué tierna mirada,
de mujer cuajada.

Alborean las mañanas frente a ti
como esos soles duros antillanos:
ríes con risa de miel
cocida en un trapiche nuevo.
Mujer hecha con levadura de la zona tórrida;
mujer hecha de piña veraniega,
tu vientre virgen moldeará los tintes
de la generación que más se riega.

MULATTO WOMAN

Juan Zapata Olivella

If only one race prevailed,
your eyes would not be dark eyes,
nor your hair, kinky hair,
nor the color of your skin
so burnished.
If the genes which conceived you
were the genes of a single race,
your slim palm-like body
would not proffer such palm tree grace.

All the hybridism of your mouth
is the sensual fruit of the tropics,
there is annatto on your Guinean lips
and that audacious malice in your glance
denounces the spirit of your native ancestry.
If we look at the map of your naked body,
all of the peoples of the world appear.
What a joy to sip a cocktail
from your breasts like Grecian amphoras!

What a firm silhouette,
what fine intelligence,
and that tender look,
of the complete woman!

The mornings dawn before you
like those harsh Antillean suns;
you laugh a laughter like honey
simmered in a new press.
Woman made with the yeast of the tropics;
woman made of summer pineapple,
your virgin womb will cast the mold
of a generation destined to be scattered.

Nuevas serán las aguas de tu llanto,
nuevas serán las células del continente;
posas sin ropas en todos los espejos
de los lagos de América.

The waters of your tears will be new,
the shape of the continent will be new;
like naked buttocks in all the mirrors
of the lakes of America.

Jorge Artel

The Afro-Colombian poet Jorge Artel has been proclaimed by the noted Hispanist, Richard L. Jackson, as one of the "staunchest literary defenders" of the black man in Colombia. According to Jackson, Artel's work, like that of a significant number of other Afro-Latin American poets, "forcefully recognize(s) that black life was characterized by suffering as well as rhythm."[16]

Artel was born in 1909 in Cartagena de Indias, a province on the Caribbean coast of Colombia, which was the scene of slave revolts as early as the first decade of the 17th century. He is well known and respected as a journalist, novelist, scholar, and diplomat.

In his extensive travels in the Americas, Artel personally observed the suffering and pain common to the black experience. This suffering became a constant theme in his poetry; especially the suffering experienced by black people in the United States.[17] "And it is through recognition of and identification with this suffering that Artel, Colombian poet, establishes rapport with his race."[18]

Artel's work *Tambores en la noche* (Drums in the Night) was first published in 1940 in Colombia and was reissued in 1956 in Mexico. The poems "Danza, Mulata","Bullerengue", and "La cumbia" are taken from this work. Of these three poems, "Bullerengue" comes closest to the elements of the popular culture, through the use of Afro-Latin American music and musical symbols. Here the protagonist expresses his praise for his black woman, while alluding to the fact that she is the sole beneficiary of his love and affection. These amorous words are expressed in the characteristic speech of the Afro-Colombian.

"Danza, Mulata" and "La cumbia", while sharing references to the rich musical heritage of Afro-Colombia, achieve a greater thematic and stylistic density. The mulatto dancer emerges as the nostalgic symbol of the black race whose aspirations rely heavily on her strength and her ability to endure.

BULLERENGUE

Jorge Artel

    Si yo fuera tambó,
mi negra,
sonara na má pa ti,
pa ti, mi negra, pa ti.

    Si maraca fuera yo,
sonara sólo para ti,
pa ti, maraca y tambó,
pa ti, mi negra, pa ti.

    Quisiera bobbebme gaita
y soná na má que pa ti,
pa ti, solita, pa ti,
pa ti, mi negra, pa ti.

"BULLERENGUE"

Jorge Artel

> If I were a drum,
> black girl,
> I would beat only for you,
> for you, black girl, for you.
>
> If I were a maraca,
> I would play only for you,
> for you, maraca and drum,
> for you, black girl, for you.
>
> I would like to be a flute,
> and play just for you,
> for you, just for you,
> for you, black girl, for you.

DANZA, MULATA

Jorge Artel

Danza, mulata, danza,
mientras canta
en el tambor de los abuelos
el son languidecente de la raza.
Alza tus manos ágiles
para apresar el aire,
envuélvete en tu cuerpo
de rugiente deseo,
donde late la queja de las gaitas
bajo el ardor de tu broncinea carne.

Deja que el sol fustigue
tu belleza demente,
que corra por tus flancos inquietantes
el ritmo que tus senos estremece.
Aprisiona en tu talle atormentado
esa música bruja
que acompasa la voz de la canción.

¡Danza, mulata, danza!
En tus piernas veloces y en el son
que han empapado tus lúbricas caderas,
doscientos siglos se agazapan.
¡Danza, mulata, danza!
Tú y yo sentimos en la sangre
galopar el incendio de una misma nostalgia...

DANCE, MULATTO

Jorge Artel

Dance, mulatto, dance,
while our grandparents' drum
sings the languid song
of our race.
Raise your agile hands
to catch the music,
wrap yourself in your body
of blushing desire,
where the lament of the bagpipe stirs
beneath the ardor of your bronze flesh.

Let the sun lash
your wild beauty,
let the rhythm that makes your breasts tremble
flow through your restless thighs.
Capture in your tormented body
that bewitching music
which measures the beat of the song.

Dance, mulatto, dance!
In your agile legs and in the rhythm
that has drenched your smooth hips,
two hundred centuries are concealed.
Dance, mulatto, dance!
You and I feel burning in our veins
the fire of the same nostalgia...

LA CUMBIA
(Fragment)

Jorge Artel

Amalgama de sombras y de luces de esperma,
la cumbia frenética,
la diabólica cumbia,
pone a cabalgar su ritmo oscuro
sobre las caderas ágiles
de las sensuales hembras.
Y la tierra,
como una axila cálida de negra,
su agrio vaho levanta, denso de temblor,
bajo los pies furiosos
que amasan golpes de tambor.

THE CUMBIA
(Fragment)

Jorge Artel

Amalgam of shadows and sperm lights,
the frenzied *cumbia*,
the diabolic *cumbia*,
begins to impose its dark rhythm
on the agile hips
of the sensuous women.
And the earth,
like the warm armpit of a black girl,
raises its pungent odor, dense with trembling,
under the furious feet
which stamp to the beat of the drum.

Notes

1. Richard L. Jackson, *Black Writers in Latin America* (Albuquerque: University of New Mexico Press, 1979), p. 55.
2. Stanley A. Cyrus, "The Development of Black Literature in Hispanic America" (Lecture), NEH Workshop, Hampton Institute, Virginia, 3 June 1978.
3. Nicolás Guillén, "Sobre Candelario Obeso," *Granma* (Havana), 12 June 1966, quoted in Richard L. Jackson, *Black Writers in Latin America*, p. 59.
4. Jackson, p. 54.
5. *zambo*, the male offspring of a black and an Indian parent.
6. Enrique Anderson Imbert, *Historia de la literatura hispanoamericana* (Mexico: Fondo de Cultura Económica, 5th ed., 1966), p. 196.
7. Anderson Imbert, p. 196.
8. Hortensia Ruiz del Vizo, *Poesía negra del Caribe y otras áreas* (Miami: Ediciones Universal, 1972), p. 135.
9. Jaime Mejia Duque, "El Chocó en la nueva poesía americana" in Hugo Salazar Valdés, *Pleamar*, p. 93.
10. Ruiz del Vizo, p. 135.
11. *guarapo*, liquor made from sugar cane.
12. Anderson Imbert, pp. 331-32.
13. Ruiz del Vizo, p. 128.
14. Ruiz del Vizo, p. 129.
15. Ruiz del Vizo, p. 102.
16. Richard L. Jackson, *The Black Image in Latin American Literature* (Albuquerque: University of New Mexico Press, 1976), p. 44.
17. Jackson, *The Black Image in Latin American Literature*, p. 118.
18. Jackson, *The Black Image in Latin American Literature*, p. 118.

ECUADOR

Adalberto Ortiz
"Antojo"
"Mosongo y la Niña Negra"
"La Tunda Para el Negrito"
"Sábado y Domingo"
"Jolgorio"
"¿Qué Tendrá la Soledad?

Nelson Estupiñán Bass
"Negra Bullanguera"
"Tú Sabías"

Adalberto Ortiz

Adalberto Ortiz, "poet, black poet, poet of black people," short story writer, novelist, literary critic, and diplomat, is a native of the province of Esmeraldas, a region of the Pacific lowlands of Ecuador. According to Ortiz, this area was settled in the early 16th century by black slaves who escaped from a Spanish galley on its way to Peru.[1] During his childhood, the writer's "spirit was nurtured by the Esmeraldian atmosphere"—"the sound of primitive musical instruments, the laughter of carefree blacks, and the clinking of fierce machetes, which were often used to sever heads as well as to farm . . ."—an atmosphere where "black men experienced pain and misery, servitude and abandon, but underneath everything, they always had a latent desire for liberation and fight."[2]

Ortiz tells us that in Esmeraldas "the black man added a distinctive and appealing folkloric note to the Ecuadorian shore with the primitive syncopated music of the marimba, bass drums, bongo drums, *guasas* and scrapers, music that could be adapted to happy celebrations, or could be used for funeral wakes by those who sang the Song of Praise and the Moonlight songs."[3] Much of this "distinctive and appealing folkloric note" of the black people of Ecuador is captured and preserved in the works of this prize-winning writer.

Economic deprivation and lack of physical strength marked and marred the early life of this writer. In the "Información del Autor" (Information about the Author) which prefaces his collection of poems entitled *El animal herido* (The Wounded Animal), Ortiz states: "It was not until I was twenty-four years old that I had a serious interest in literature. I was more interested in sports, and I would have liked to excel in them; but a certain lack of physical vigor made that impossible. It was not a case of being crippled or anything like that, but rather the fact of growing up in a family which was economically deprived made it impossible for me to be physically strong and vigorous."[4] Ortiz explains that his interest in literature was aroused in 1937 when he read the *Antología de la poesía negra americana* (Anthology of Black American Poetry) compiled by the Cuban Emilio Ballagas. Ortiz began to observe and "live the folklore of Esmeraldas."[5] From these observations and experiences originate his poetic works: *Tierra, son y tambor* (Land, Sound, and Drum), published in 1940; *Camino y puerto de la angustia* (Anguish's Way), 1945; *El vigilante insepulto* (The Unburied Watchman), 1957; and *El animal herido* (The Wounded Animal), 1959.

Adalberto Ortiz won the 1942 Premio Nacional de la Novela for his novel *Juyungo*. A later novel, *El espejo y la ventana* (The Mirror and the Window) also won a national prize in 1964. His short stories include *La mala espalda* (Evil Fate), 1952; *La entundada y cuentos variados* (The Girl Who Was Bewitched by the Tunda and Other Stories), 1971. His play, "El retrato de la otra" (Portrait of the Other Woman) received its first production in 1970.

The poems which follow are all taken from Ortiz's collection *Tierra, son y tambor*. The poet describes the pain and rejection suffered by black women in the white world ("Antojo"); the joys of contemplating a beautiful black girl ("Mosongo y la niña negra"); a mother affirming African culture ("La tunda para el negrito"); the exuberance and spontaneity of blacks dancing to the rhythms of traditional African music ("Sábado y domingo" and "Jolgorio"); and the melancholy mood of the black woman Soledad.

ANTOJO

Adalberto Ortiz

¡Ay, mamá, yo quiero un blanco!
Un blanco yo quiero, mamá.
Compráme también un frasco,
un frasco de Agua'e Kananga.
Un blanco que tenga un tongo,
un tongo de plata, mamá.

Que sepa leé y escribí,
pa que me diga cositas
que no saben los de aquí.
¡Ay, mama, yo quiero un gringo!
Un gringo muy colorao,
que tenga lo'sojo lindo
como cielo despejao.

Mucho pedís, muchacha,
negra conga y presumía,
negra conga y má pincháa
no hei visto en toa mi vía.

Er blanco que tú queré,
te lo puedo seguí;
pero luego vamo a vé
si te quiere solo a ti.

Er blanco te coge, negra,
como una curiosidá
y cuando meno lo piensas
te va dejando botáa.
Er blanco te va'empreñá,
er blanco te va a pateá.

CAPRICE

Adalberto Ortiz

Ay, mama, I want a white man!
A white man is what I want, mama.
Also I want you to buy me a flask,
a flask of Kananga water.
And a white man who has a big wad,
a roll of money, mama.

One who knows how to read and write
so that he can tell me things
that the men around here don't know.
Ay mama, I want a *gringo*!
A very ruddy *gringo*,
who has pretty eyes
like a clear sky.

You want a lot, *muchacha*,
uppity black Conga girl,
a more uppity black Conga girl
I ain't never seen in my life.

The white man that you want,
I can get him for you;
but later we'll just see
if he'll be faithful to you.

That white man will take you, girl
for some kind of oddity
and before you know it
he'll just up and leave you.
The white man will get you pregnant,
and he's sure to kick you around.

Si te juntá con un blanco,
tu'sijo son casi negro,
tu'sijo son casi blanco.
Tu'sijo ya no son náa.

¡Ay! Ya no quiero gringo,
no quiero, mamá.
¡Ay! Ya no quiero blanco,
no quiero, mamá.

Sólo quiero negro,
mi negro quiero.

If you get hooked up with a white man,
your children will be almost black,
your children will be almost white.
Your children won't be nothing.

Ay! I don't want a *gringo* no more,
I don't want one, mama.
Ay! I don't want a white man no more,
I don't want him, mama.

I only want a black man,
I'll love my black man.

MOSONGO Y LA NIÑA NEGRA

Adalberto Ortiz

Vestida de verde va
una joven de azabache:
del ébano el corazón
es la fibra de su carne,
con movimientos de mar
y temblores de cazabe.
Los labios de marañón,
los senos de chocolate,
su linda risa es de cal,
de caña brava su talle,
y tersura hay en su piel
como en la flor de la tarde.

Quien en la calle la vio,
de ella no quiso olvidarse;
quien la ha sacado a bailar,
quiere estar en todo baile.
Todos arden por saber
el secreto de su carne.
Sus amigas, las de allá,
hasta han llegado a envidiarle.
De sus miradas de sol
nadie ha sabido escaparse.

De ser negra como es
no han podido avergonzarle;
pero hasta ahora su amor
a nadie ha querido darle.
¿Para quién ella será?
Ella misma no lo sabe.
¿Será de un blanco tal vez?
Quién sabe, negra, quién sabe.
De un negro serías mejor,
vestida de verde cade.

MOSONGO AND THE BLACK GIRL

Adalberto Ortiz

    Jet black girl
    dressed in green,
    heart of ebony
    the fiber of her flesh,
    wave-like movements
    trembling like cassava.
    Cashew lips.
    Chocolate breasts,
    fine white teeth,
    sugar cane figure,
    and skin as smooth
    as an afternoon flower.

    If you see her on the street,
    you can't forget her;
    if you dance with her,
    you'll want to dance forever.
    All men long to know
    the secret of her flesh.
    Her friends, other women,
    even envy her now.
    From her sunny glances
    no one has escaped.

    Even being as black as she is
    no one can make her ashamed;
    she has not yet
    given her love to anyone.
    Who is she waiting for?
    Even she cannot say.
    Will it be a white man?
    Who knows, black girl, who knows.
    Give your love to a black man
    (black girl) dressed in green.

LA TUNDA PARA EL NEGRITO

Adalberto Ortiz

Portáte bien, mi morito,
pa que yo to dé café.
Porque si viene la tunda,
la tunda te va a cogé.

No te escondás, mi negrito,
que ya te voy a buscá.
Y si la tunda te encuentra,
la tunda te va a entundá.

Pa duro te toy criando,
y no pa flojo ¿sabé?
Y si te agarra la tunda,
la tunda te va a mordé.

Cuando llegués a sé hombre
vos tenés que trabajá.
Porque si viene la tunda,
la tunda te va a llevá.

No quiero que seas un bruto,
sino que sepás leé.
Que si te agarra la tunda,
la tunda te va a comé.

y no te dejés de naide,
respetáme sólo a mí.
Porque ya viene la tunda,
la tunda ya va a veni.

Echáte pronto en tu magua,
que no te voy a pegá.
¡Huy! Que ya llega la tunda!
¡La tunda ya va a llegá!

BOGEY MAN FOR A LITTLE BLACK BOY

Adalberto Ortiz

Behave yourself, my little Moor,
and I'll give you a little coffee.
Because if the *tunda* comes,
the *tunda* is going to get you.

Don't hide from me, my little black boy,
because I'm going to look for you.
And if the *tunda* finds you,
the *tunda* is going to jinx you.

I'm raising you to be a strong man,
and not a weak one, you hear?
And if the *tunda* catches you,
the *tunda* is going to bite you.

When you get to be a man
you will have to get a job.
But if the *tunda* comes,
the *tunda* is going to take you away.

I don't want you to be dumb,
I want you to learn how to read.
For if the *tunda* snatches you,
the *tunda* is going to eat you up.

Don't let anyone be your master,
give your respect only to me.
Because if the *tunda* comes...
The *tunda* is coming now.

Go to bed right this minute,
I'm not going to spank you.
Whew! Here comes the *tunda*!
The *tunda* is arriving right now!

SÁBADO Y DOMINGO

Adalberto Ortiz

¡Marimba en barrio caliente!
Vamos pa'llá, mano Fuan.
Mirá, ya pasa la gente,
todos pá'l baile van.

Se oyen tiros de trabuco...
Fijáte qué penco de hembra
tá bailando el Bambuco,
y pa mové la gurupa:
¡ayayaay...!

Qué negra tan mamaú.
"Mi sombrero grande,
mi verejú."
Torbellino tocá,
Andariele cantá.
marimbero, marimbero,
echalé con más amó.
Torbellino tocá.
Caderona cantá.

Qué blanca tu yampa,
mano Migué.
Fijáte en la blanca,
mano Fidé.
Mové ligero tu pie
que los blancos te quieren vé.
Bebéte otro trago má
que e'lunes a trabajá...

Véle la jeta a ese negro,
qué negro tan balambá.
Mejó me fijo en mi negra,
qué negra tan mamaú.

SATURDAY AND SUNDAY

Adalberto Ortiz

>Hot marimba in the *barrio*!
>Let's go, Bro Fuan.
>Look at the folks on their way,
>all going to the dance.
>
>Listen to the fireworks...
>Look at that fine girl
>dancing the *Bambuco*,[6]
>and when she moves her rump:
>ayayaay...!
>
>What a pretty black girl.
>"My big hat,
>my devil."
>Play Torbellino,
>Sing Andariele.
>Marimba player,
>play it more sweetly.
>Play Torbellino.
>Sing Caderona.
>
>What a white jacket you have,
>Bro Migue.
>Look at that white girl,
>Bro Fide.
>Move those feet of yours
>'cause the white folks want to see you.
>Have another drink
>'cause Monday is a work day...
>
>Look at that Negro's thick lips,
>what a rough black fellow.
>I'd rather look at my black girl,
>what a fine black girl.

"Mi sombrero grande,
mi verejú.
Mi sombrero grande,
mi verejú."

"My big hat,
my devil.
My big hat,
my devil."

JOLGORIO

Adalberto Ortiz

Está vomitando el bombo
su enorme bom.
Cununo que cununea:
taca, taca tom;
taca-taca tomb
Arrulla la guacharaca:
chaca, chaca, guasá.
Risa de un palitroque:
taraca, taracatá.
Va la marimba a soná:
tucu, tucu, tunn,
tucu, tucu, tunn,
tucu, tucu, tunn.

Canta un negro renegro,
venido del Telembí:
Zambambé, zambambú,
cachimba, cacherimbá.
Negrito caracumbé,
saca cuchillo, matá mujé.
Upapé, jajejá,
aé, aú.

Seguí cantando nomá,
que el negro no baila tango,
el negro tan sólo baila
carioca, marimba y rumba;
batuque, marimba y bomba.

Mamapunga, sudor,
tabaco y luz de candil;
patas de negro que suenan
sobre el pambil.

FROLIC

Adalberto Ortiz

>The bass drum releases
>its enormous *bom.*
>*Cununo* drum that beats:
>*taca, taca, tom;*
>*taca-taca tomb.*
>The *guacharaca* hums:[7]
>*chaca, chaca, guasá.*
>Laughter of the drum stick:
>*taraca, taracatá.*
>The marimba will play:
>*tucu, tucu, tunn,*
>*tucu, tucu, tunn,*
>*tucu, tucu, tunn.*
>
>A jet black Negro
>from Telembi sings:
>*Zambambé, zambambú,*
>*cachimba, cacherimbá*[8]
>*Caracumbé* Negro,
>takes out his knife, "kills" a woman.
>*Upapé, jajejá,*
>*aé, aú.*
>
>I kept on saying
>that the Negro doesn't tango,
>the Negro only dances
>*carioca, marimba* and *rumba;*
>*baruque, marimba* and *bomba.*[9]
>
>Cane whiskey, sweat,
>tobacco and lamp light;
>black feet that resound
>on the palm-wood floor.

Los senos, la rabadilla
y el vientre bajo
que se emborracha con el olor.
Qué zamba pa tené bemba,
metéle una zancadilla.
Zumbále el mango,
zumbále el mango.
Gira cabeza pamba,
brilla machete yambo,
que corta cambo,
que corta cambo.

Patas negras del mundo
que sólo bailan:
batuque, marimba y rumba.
Bembas de negros que cantan:
candombe, marimba y conga.

The breasts, the buttocks
and the low belly
which the fragrance intoxicates.
What a black girl to have thick lips,
play a trick on her.
Zumbále el mango,
zumbále el mango.[10]
She turns her flat head,
the flat machete glistens,
which cuts banana trees,
which cuts banana trees.

Black feet of the world
which only dance:
batuque, marimba and *rumba.*
Thick lips of Negroes who sing:
candombe, marimba and *conga.*

¿QUÉ TENDRÁ LA SOLEDAD?

Adalberto Ortiz

Toca que toca el guasá.
¿Quién?
La mulata Soledá.

Canta la Caramba, caramba.
Baila la Caramba, caramba.

Sentada sobre un cununo,
triste, qué triste está ya.
Vagos los ojos oscuros,
parecen de enamoráa.

Se oye una Agualarga, lejana.
Suena una Aguacorta, temprana.
Cuando del baile se va,
¿qué se hará la Soledá?
Llorá, no má que llorá.

WHAT'S THE MATTER WITH SOLEDAD?

Adalberto Ortiz

    Listen how she plays the *guasá*[11]
       Who?
    The mulatto Soledá.

    She sings the *Caramba, caramba*.
    She dances the *Caramba, caramba*. [12]

    Seated on a drum,
    sad, how sad she is.
    Vague dark eyes
    of a woman in love.

    An *Agualarga* is heard, far away.
    An *Aguacorta* is played, nearby.[13]
    When she leaves the dance,
    what will become of Soledá?
    She'll cry, she'll just cry.

Nelson Estupiñán Bass

The province of Esmeraldas claims as its own another important Afro-Ecuadorian writer, Nelson Estupiñán Bass. Born in 1912, Estupiñán is well known as a poet, novelist, short story writer, and political activist and has been described by Stanley Cyrus as "one of the greatest virtues of Ecuadorian literature."[14]

Like his compatriot Adalberto Ortiz and the white novelists of the "Group of Guayaquil" (Demetrio Aguilera Malta, Joaquín Gallegos Lara, José de la Cuadra, Enrique Gil Gilbert, and Alfredo Pareja Diez-Canseco), Estupiñán is "in the forefront of the literary redeemers of the black in Latin America. In coming to his defense thay have laid bare the evils of racial prejudice, discrimination, and exploitation while portraying the black as a proud, rebellious type not reluctant to fight for his own social and political betterment."[15]

In his essay "Negritude in Latin American Culture", Adalberto Ortiz writes: "It was only at the end of the Thirties that the poet and novelist Nelson Estupiñán Bass and I began to write Negrist poetry, novels and short stories in the Caribbean manner, using, however, our own elements and materials to give our work a national flavor. Beginning in the Forties, we wrote novels and some short stories with the black theme."[16]

Estupiñán's works include the novels *Cuando los guayacanes florecían* (When the Guaiacum Bloomed), 1954; *El paraíso* (Paradise), 1958; *El último río* (The Last River), 1967; and *El negro y el río* (The Black Man and the River). His published collections of poetry include *Canto negro por la luz* (Black Song for the Light), 1954; *Timarán y Cuabú*, 1956; and *Las huellas digitales* (Fingerprints), 1971.

The poems "Negra bullanguera" (Wild Black Girl) and "Tú sabias . . ." (You Knew . . .), which follow, are taken from *Canto negro por la luz*. The black women of these two poems, although presented as wild and bewitching pleasure-givers, are imbued with a more profound and more lasting significance when they are characterized as bearers of future sons and daughters who will raise their "black fists" in rebellion against the suffering and misfortunes of their race.

NEGRA BULLANGUERA

Nelson Estupiñán Bass

Negra, negra bullanguera,
negra; juyunga, cuscunga,
tu boca anoche me supo
a un mate de agua surumba.

Negra, negra bullanguera,
negra, juyunga, cuscunga,
hacé callá tu cadera,
dejá tranquila mi vida.

Negra, negra bullanguera,
negra, juyunga, cuscunga
en la calle tu cadera
se cimbra como escalera.

Negra, negra bullanguera,
negra, juyunga, cuscunga,
de caderas de pantera,
te voy a hacé esta propuesta
por rebelde y altanera:
tengamos los dos un hijo
pa que cuando yo me muera
sus puños color de brea
conduzcan nuestra bandera.

WILD BLACK GIRL

Nelson Estupiñán Bass

> Black girl, wild black girl,
> black, jet black, bewitching girl,
> last night your lips tasted
> like tea made with sugar water.
>
> Black girl, wild black girl,
> black, jet black, bewitching girl,
> still your swaying hips,
> and leave me in peace.
>
> Black girl, wild black girl,
> black, jet black, bewitching girl,
> on the streets, your hips
> go up and down like steps.
>
> Black girl, wild black girl,
> black, jet black, bewitching girl,
> with panther-like hips,
> I am going to make you a proposition
> at once outlandish and arrogant:
> let's have a child together
> so that when I die
> his black fists
> will carry forth our banner.

TÚ SABÍAS...

Nelson Estupiñán Bass

Tú sabías
que día y noche
mi sangre insomne te acechaba.
Que mis brazos anhelantes
te perseguían sin tregua por todos los caminos.
Que mi sangre
que había profanado los templos
—ah, yo siempre me río del frontispicio de las iglesias!—
se había alzado tumultuosa
por sobre los miserables mandamientos de las esclusas.

Tú sabías también
de esta angustia sin rumbo que milita en mi sangre,
que viene desde el fondo inmemorial de mis primeros días,
y que hablando con el lenguaje de mis manos
buscaba un bloque de roca selvática
para tallar dos puños negros
que un día levantarán nuestras banderas amortajadas
aquí en estos sitios,
eternamente verdes e indómitos.

Tal vez la culpa estuvo:

en tu cuerpo magnético,
negro como los pliegues de la noche en el corazón enredado de las selvas,
donde los ofidios, por el sueño,
dejan evaporar sus alcaloides
y las fieras cuelgan sus garras
en las ramas borrosas del sopor.

En tu cuerpo, elástico como una guadúa verde,
ágil como la risotada de un niño,
meciéndose siempre en el columpio incesante del deseo.

YOU KNEW...

Nelson Estupiñán Bass

You knew
that day and night
my restless blood longed for you.
That my anxious arms
sought you ceaselessly everywhere you went.
That my blood
which had profaned the temples
—how I always laughed at the facades of churches!—
had risen up defiantly
over the wretched commandments of the floodgates.

You also knew
about this pervasive anxiety that courses through my blood,
which comes from the timeless depths of my childhood,
and that speaking with the language of my hands
I searched for a slab of pristine rock
with which to fashion two black fists
which one day will raise high our shrouded banner
here in this place
eternally verdant and untamed.

Perhaps the blame lies:

in the magnetism of your body,
as black as the folds of night in the thick heart of the jungle,
where the ophidians, in the throes of sleep,
permit their vital juices to evaporate
and the wild beasts hang their claws
on the muddled branches of sleep.

In your body, as elastic as a green bamboo,
as sprightly as the raucous laughter of a child,
rocking himself in the incessant swing of desire.

Notes

1. Adalberto Ortiz, "Negritude in Latin American Culture," in Miriam DeCosta, *Blacks in Hispanic Literature* (Port Washington, NY: Kennikat Press, 1977), p. 77.
2. Ortiz, pp. 76-77.
3. Ortiz, p. 78.
4. Adalberto Ortiz, *El animal herido* (Quito: Editorial Casa de la Cultura Ecuatoriana, 1970), p. 7.
5. Ortiz, *El animal herido*, p. 7.
6. *bambuco,* Colombian dance.
7. *guacharaca*, musical instrument, sometimes called *guasá*, made from a piece of bamboo filled with seeds or stones.
8. "Zambambé, zambambú/cachimba, cacherimba". Onomatopoeic words.
9. "carioca, marimba, rumba;/batuque, marimba, bomba". Afro-Latin American dance music, usually played on the marimba. The *bomba* is a typical dance of the blacks who inhabit the mountainous regions of Ecuador, Minda, and Chota.
10. "Zúmbale el mango", "Zumbarle el mango a alguien" is an exaggerated expression of the value of someone. Here it probably means, "Lavish her with praise."
11. *guasá*, see note 7.
12. *La Caramba*, musical selection played on the marimba.
13. *Agualarga* and *aguacorta*, musical selections played on the marimba.
14. Stanley Cyrus, *El cuento negrista sudamericano* (Quito: Editorial Casa de la Cultura Ecuatoriana, 1973), p. 103.
15. Richard L. Jackson, *The Black Image in Latin American Literature* (Albuquerque: University of New Mexico Press, 1976), p. 84.
16. Ortiz, "Negritude in Latin American Culture," p. 79.

PERU

Nicomedes Santa Cruz
"No Es Delito Enamorar"
"Ritmos Negros del Perú"
"Como Has Cambiado, Pelona"
"Que Mi Sangre Se Sancoche"
"Día de la Madre"

Nicomedes Santa Cruz

Poet, musician, folklorist, journalist, choreographer, and short story writer, Nicomedes Santa Cruz Gamarra was born in Lima, Peru on June 4, 1925. This internationally-known member of a family of distinguished artists and writers began composing poems at the age of 24. Having pursued various careers in journalism, Peruvian folklore, poetry, public relations, advertising, and as founder in 1959 of the repertory dance company Compañia Cumanana, Santa Cruz is perhaps "the most prominent twentieth century Afro-Peruvian."[1]

Santa Cruz is "dedicated to the preservation and cultivation of black culture, folklore and music in his country."[2] His popular poetry continues a centuries-old tradition of Hispanic-American poets in his utilization of and preference for the octosyllabic line and the *copla* or the *dècima* (ten-lined stanza). As suggested by Teresa Salas and Henry Richards, Santa Cruz is a follower of the *decimistas* of the coastal area of Peru, black poets who "expressed in verse their most intimate feelings about the difficult period of acculturation. In this way, in their *dècimas* they portrayed faithfully their history, as well as the nostalgia for their native land, the rhythms of their dances, their religious practices, their syncretic cosmic vision—their cultural legacy."[3]

Santa Cruz has created some four thousand *dècimas* which have been collected and recollected, and published in the volumes *Dècimas*, 1960; *Cumanana*, 1964; *Canto a mi Perù* (A Poem to My Peru), 1966; *Antología: Dècimas y poemas*, 1971; and *Ritmos negros del Perù* (Black Rhythms of Peru), 1971. He has also recorded his poetry: *Canto negro* (Black Song), 1968 and *Cumanana: Antología afro-peruana.*

Generally accepted by literary critics and historians as the foremost representative of negritude in Peru, Santa Cruz's work is characterized by popularism and authenticity.[4] The popular elements which pervade his work and that of other South Americn poets are inspired by the common speech of black people and by their past and present experiences, often plagued by racially motivated social injustices.

In his treatment of black women, the poet variously ridicules her abandonment of the customs and traditions of her African heritage ("Como has cambiado, Pelona"); eulogizes her for surviving, with dignity, the cruel rigors of enslavement ("Ritmos negros del Perù"); playfully chides her unfaithfulness to her husband ("No es delito enamorar"); challenges her to accept the amorous longings of the male protagonist ("Que mi sangre se sancoche"); and reveres her maternal role in "Día de la madre".

NO ES DELITO ENAMORAR

Nicomedes Santa Cruz

La vida, como es tan corta
hay que saberla vivir
para más tarde decir
"Soy viejo pero qué importa."
Si el placer que más conforta
es el delirio de amar,
pues entonces a gozar
que el amor no es prohibido,
y siendo correspondido
no es delito enamorar.

Sucede frecuentemente
que con muy buena intención
se acepte la invitación
de un amigo o un pariente.
Tú llegas y él está ausente,
su mujer quiere contigo,
y no tienes más testigo
que tu cochina conciencia
para tratar con decencia
a la mujer de un amigo.

Si desprecias la ocasión,
la mujer, muerta de ira
inventa alguna mentira
y te acusa de traición.
El marido, con razón,
te toma por su enemigo
y recibes en castigo
la censura de la gente.
Nadie cree al inocente,
por experiencia les digo.

IT'S NOT A CRIME TO FALL IN LOVE

Nicomedes Santa Cruz

Since life is so very short
you have to know how to live it
so that later on you can say
"I may be old but what of it"...
If your greatest pleasure
is the excitement of loving,
well, go on and enjoy it,
for love is not prohibited,
and when it is returned,
it's not a crime to fall in love.

It frequently happens
that with the best of intentions
you accept an invitation
from a friend or a relation.
You arrive and he's not there,
his wife makes a pass at you,
and there's no other witness
than your own lowly conscience
to the way you treat
the wife of a friend.

If you do not accept her offer
the wife, mad as a hornet,
invents some damning lie
and even accuses you of treachery.
The husband, with good reason,
will consider you his enemy
and you will get as punishment
the censure of other people.
No one believes an innocent man;
I tell you that from experience.

En cambio, si tienes maña
para ponerle los cuernos,
serán amigos eternos
y si no te ve te extraña.
Mientras su mujer lo engaña
él se marcha a trabajar;
y te puedes acostar,
te puedes probar su ropa
te puedes tomar su sopa
que él nunca se ha de enterar...

But if you are clever enough
to pull the wool over his eyes,
you will be friends forever.
He'll even miss you if you're not around.
As long as his wife deceives him
he'll go off gleefully to work;
and you can climb in his bed
you can wear his clothes
you can eat his food
and he never has to know...

RITMOS NEGROS DEL PERÚ

A don Porfirio Vásquez A.

Nicomedes Santa Cruz

Ritmos de la esclavitud
contra amarguras y penas.
Al compás de las cadenas
ritmos negros del Perú.

...y dice asi:

De Africa llegó mi abuela
vestida con caracoles,
la trajeron lo'epañoles
en un barco carabela.
La marcaron con candela,
la carimba fue su cruz.
Y en América del Sur
al golpe de sus dolores
dieron los negros tambores
ritmos de la esclavitud.

Por una moneda sola
la revendieron en Lima
y en la Hacienda "La Molina"
sirvió a la gente española.
Con otros negros de Angola
ganaron por sus faenas
zancudos para sus venas
para dormir duro suelo
y naita'e consuelo
contra amarguras y penas...

En la plantación de caña
nació el triste socabón,
en el trapiche de ron
el negro cantó la zaña.

THE BLACK RHYTHMS OF PERU

To Don Porfirio Vasquez A.

Nicomedes Santa Cruz

Rhythms of slavery,
lives of pain and suffering.
To the beat of the chains,
black rhythms of Peru.

... and it goes like this:

My grandmother came from Africa
dressed in (snail) shells,
brought by the Spaniards
in a caravel boat.
They branded her with fire,
this brand was her burden.
And in South America
to the beat of her sufferings
the cruel drums beat out
rhythms of slavery.

For only a single coin
they sold her again in Lima
and on "La Molina" ranch
she waited on Spanish people.
With other blacks from Angola
her labor earned her
varicose veins
a hard floor to sleep on
and not a bit of consolation
for her harsh life and suffering.

On the sugar cane plantation
the sad *socabón was born.*[5]
In the rum factories
the black man sang the *zaña*.[6]

El machete y la guadaña
curtió sus manos morenas;
y los indios con sus quenas
y el negro con tamborete
cantaron su triste suerte
al compás de las cadenas.

Murieron los negros viejos
pero entre la caña seca
se escucha su zamacueca
y el panalivio muy lejos.
Y se escuchan los festejos
que cantó en su juventud.
De Cañete a Tombuctú,
de Chancay a Mozambique
llevan sus claros repiques
ritmos negros del Perú.

The machete and the scythe
hardened his brown hands;
and the Indians with their flutes
and the black man with his timbrel
sang of their sad fate
to the rhythm of their chains.

The old black men died
but amid the dry cane
their *zamacueca*[7] is heard
far off with the *panalivio*.[8]
And the merry songs which
they sang in their youth ring out.
From Cañete to Timbuktu
from Chancay to Mozambique
their clear sounds peal out:
the black rhythms of Peru.

COMO HAS CAMBIADO, PELONA

Nicomedes Santa Cruz

Como has cambiado, pelona,
cisco de carbonería.
Te has vuelto una negra mona
con tanta huachafería.

Te cambiaste las chancletas
por zapatos taco aguja,
y tu cabeza de bruja
la amarraste con peinetas.
Por no engordar sigues dietas
y estás flaca y hocicona.
Imitando a tu patrona
has aprendido a fumar.
Hasta en el modo de andar
como has cambiado, pelona.

Usas reloj de pulsera
y no sabes ver la hora.
Cuando un negro te enamora
le tiras con la cartera.
¡Que!....¿también usas polvera?
Permite que me sonría.
¿Que polvos se pone usía?:
¿ocre?, ¿rosado?, ¿rachel?
¿o le pones a tu piel
cisco de carbonería?

Te pintaste hasta el meñique
porque un blanco te miró.
"Francica, botá frifró
que son comé venarique!..."
Perdona que te critique,
y si me río, perdona.

HOW YOU'VE CHANGED, BALDY

Nicomedes Santa Cruz

My, how you've changed, baldy,
coal dust from the coal yard.
You've become a "cute" black girl
putting on so many airs.

So you exchanged your sandals
for some high-heeled shoes,
and your head of nappy hair
you keep plastered down with combs.
You're on a diet, not to get fat
and now you're all skin and bones.
Trying to be Miss Ann
you had to learn how to smoke.
And even in the way you walk
my, how you've changed, baldy.

You've got on a wristwatch
yet you can't even tell time.
When a black man tries to talk to you
you throw your pocketbook at him.
What? ... Do you also wear powder?
Please forgive me if I smile.
What color powder for my lady?
Is it flesh? Pink? Rachel?
Or do you powder your face
with the soot from a coal yard?

All painted up, from head to toe
'cause a white man looked your way.
"Francica, throw out the beans
'cause we gonna eat venison! ..."
Forgive me for criticizing.
If I laugh, do pardon me.

Antes eras tan pintona
con tu traje de percala
y hoy, por dártela de mala,
te has vuelto una negra mona.

Deja ese estilo bellaco.
Vuelve a ser la misma de antes.
Menos polvos, menos guantes,
menos humo de tabaco.
Vuelve con tu negro flaco
que te adora todavía.
Y si no, la policía
te va a llevar de la jeta
por dártela de coqueta
con tanta huachafería.

Before, you were so fresh-looking
with your simple cotton dress
and now, by changing your ways
you have become a "cute" black girl.

Forget all these silly ways,
be what you were before.
Use less powder, fewer gloves,
and smoke fewer cigarettes.
Come back to your skinny black man
who still loves you very much.
And if you don't, the policeman
will drag you away by your snout
for playing the part of a coquette,
putting on all those airs.

QUE MI SANGRE SE SANCOCHE

Nicomedes Santa Cruz

Que mi sangre se sancoche
en el ron de la jarana,
y que me sirvan más noche
en mi copa de mañana.

Negra, grupa de repisa,
cinturita de cuchara.
En la noche de tu cara
hay media luna de risa.
Esta noche tienes prisa
por provocar algún boche.
Me miras como en reproche,
con todo el cuerpo me miras
y deseas cuando giras
que mi sangre se sancoche.

Vas a salir con tu gusto
y sea lo que Dios quiera,
porque en esta marinera
contra tu pecho me ajusto.
A ver si me mata el susto
o tu carne palangana.
Y a ver si me da la gana
de probarle el chivillo
que yo templé mi cuchillo
en el ron de la jarana...

La lengua del lamparín
lamió sus labios de vidrio,
tras un estertor de iridio
calló, bostezando hollín.
Luz neón de un cafetín
fue el alba de mi derroche:

LET MY BLOOD RUN HOT

Nicomedes Santa Cruz

Let my blood run hot
on the rum of revelry,
and serve me more darkness
in my morning cup.

Black girl, with a big rump,
waist the size of a spoon.
In the darkness of your face
there's a half-moon smile.
Tonight you're trying your best
to get a rise out of me.
You look at me with reproach,
your whole body looks at me
but as you dance you want
to stir up my blood.

You can have your own way
and may it be as God wills
for while dancing this *marinera*,[9]
I'll snuggle against your breast.
Will it be my fear which kills me
or your foolish sensuality?
And just in case I might want
to experience your black skin
I have tempered my knife
in the rum of revelry.

The wick of the lantern
licked its crystal-like lips,
after a rattling sound,
it became still, yawning lamp black.
The neon light of a small café
was the dawn of my wantoness

—Mozo, toma y busca un broche
donde colgar mi tristeza,
y luego limpia esta mesa
y que me sirvan más noche!...

Negra... grupa de repisa,
cintura de cuchara...
La hazaña me costó cara,
tu gente pega y no avisa.
Me han abierto en la camisa
un ojal de color grana...
Sigue, negra palangana,
que esta noche voy de nuevo,
y me matan o te bebo
en mi copa de mañana

—Waiter, come and find a hanger
where I can hang my sadness,
and afterwards clean this table
and serve me more blackness.

Black girl... with your big rump,
spoon-sized waist...
That act cost me dearly,
your family attacked without warning.
They made a hole in my shirt
the color of scarlet grain.
Keep it up, foolish black girl,
because tonight I'll be back,
either they kill me or I'll have you
in my morning cup.

DÍA DE LA MADRE

Nicomedes Santa Cruz

Este domingo de mayo
vergüenza debiera darme:
Marcar un día del año
para querer a la madre...

Tomar del día una hora,
de la hora unos instantes;
y con un ramo de flores
y unos versos miserables,
y con un beso en la frente
creer pagar lo impagable...

Este domingo de mayo
vergüenza debiera darme.

Que haya un "Día de la Raza"
lo acepto por segregarme,
como acepto sin disfraz
un día de Carnavales:
y acepto el "Día del Indio"
y acepto el "Día del Padre"
y hasta el "Día del Idioma"
en memoria de Cervantes.
Pero me apena que exista
sólo un "Día" de la madre
cuando toda una existencia
no basta para adorarle...

Este domingo de Mayo
vergüenza debiera darme.

Deben haberlo creado
para esos pobres hogares
donde el amor lo recuerda
lo rojo del almanaque.

MOTHER'S DAY

Nicomedes Santa Cruz

This Sunday in May
should make me feel ashamed.
To single out one day a year
to honor and love my mother...

To take from the day an hour,
from the hour a few minutes;
and with a bouquet of flowers
and with a few hollow verses,
and with a kiss on the forehead
attempt to repay the unpayable...

This Sunday in May
should make me feel ashamed.

That there is a "Day of the Race";
I accept it and stay away,
the way I accept Carnival
without wearing a costume,
and I accept "Indian Day"
and I accept "Father's Day"
and even "Spanish Day"
in memory of Cervantes.
But it grieves me to have only
one "Day" to honor our mothers
when a whole lifetime
would not suffice to pay them homage...

This Sunday in May
should make me feel ashamed.

It must have been created
for those wretched homes
where love is remembered
by marking it on the calendar.

O quizás para esos hijos
que acarician con postales
a la que les dio la vida
con llanto, sudor y sangre...

Este domingo de mayo
vergüenza debiera darme.

Marcar el día, la hora,
premeditar el instante.
Inventar un día al año
para querer a la madre...

Este domingo de mayo
vergüenza debiera darme.

Or perhaps for those children
who, with greeting cards,
embrace the one who gave them life
with her blood, sweat and tears...

This Sunday in May
should make me feel ashamed.

To set aside the day, the hour,
to designate the moment.
To invent a day of the year
to love one's mother...

This Sunday in May
should make me feel ashamed.

Notes

[1] Leslie B. Rout, Jr., *The African Experience in Spanish America: 1502 to the Present Day* (Cambridge University Press, 1976), p. 225.

[2] Richard L. Jackson, *The Black Image in Latin American Literature* (Albuquerque: University of New Mexico Press, 1976), p. 111.

[3] Teresa C. Salas and Henry J. Richards, "Nicomedes Santa Cruz y la poesía de su conciencia de negritud," *Cuadernos Americanos* (September-October 1975), 182.

[4] Stanley Cyrus, *El cuento negrista sudamericano* (Quito: Editorial Casa de la Cultura Ecuatoriana, 1973), p. 33.

[5] *socabón*, guitar melody, played to accompany the 10th stanza of a song in the tradition of the Peruvian coast. (Enrique Noble, *Literatura afrohispanoamericana* (Lexington, Massachusetts: Xerox, 1973), p. 37.

[6] *zaña*, dance performed by the black slaves of the Zaña region in Peru.

[7] *zamacueca*, song and dance typical of the Peruvian mestizo culture which today is known as *marinera*.

[8] *panalivio*, work song of the Peruvian blacks; a lament.

[9] *marinera*, see note 7.

URUGUAY

Virginia Brindis de Salas   "Aleluya"
"Semblanza"
"Madrigal"
"La Conga"
"Unguet"
"Pregón Número Uno"
"Pregón Número Dos"

Gastón Figueira   "Quitandeira"

Pilar E. Barrios   "Poema de la Madre"
"Negra"

Virginia Brindis de Salas

Uruguay, a land which boasts of its female poets, especially the triad of María Eugenia Vaz Ferreira, Delmira Agustini, and Juana de Ibarbourou, has virtually ignored one of its rare black feminine voices, Virginia Brindis de Salas. Although little is known of the intellectual influences on Brindis de Salas, her observations on, concern for, and protest of the harsh reality of the lives of her black compatriots are well documented in her two volumes of poetry, *Pregón de Marimorena* (The Call of Marimorena), 1947; and *Cien cárceles de amor* (One Hundred Prisons of Love), 1949.

Richard L. Jackson suggests another triad of Uruguayan literati of more relevance to this study, three outstanding black poet-journalists who have used journalism and poetry as their "main vehicles of expression . . . to take their ideas to the public": Virginia Brindis de Salas, Pilar Barrios, and the lesser-known Juan Julio Arrascaeta, who, together with Julio Guadalupe and others, collaborated in the publication of the journal "Nuestra Raza" (Our Race), in the late thirties and forties.[1]

Julio Guadalupe, prologuist of Brindis de Salas' first published work, *Pregón de Marimorena*, from which selections for this anthology have been taken, praises the poet for rejecting the "sentimental timidity" of the majority of Latin American women poets. He appreciates Brindis de Salas' refusal to follow in the footsteps of the Uruguayans Agustini and Vaz Ferreira and of the Argentinian poet Alfonsina Storni, who were immersed in a kind of "personal romanticism."[2]

Indeed, the strong, black poetic voice of Virginia Brindis de Salas is steeped not in romanticism but in a "new realism" which loudly affirms her pride in her African heritage. Her poetry "is very much in the mainstream of the literature by Latin American writers of African descent because of her forceful presentation of the black experience in America; for her awareness of her African heritage invoked in allusions, African-sounding works and rhythms in Spanish . . . and largely because of the revolutionary impact that her verses . . . have made on black readers."[3]

Her poems about the black woman reflect her desire to portray her subjects realistically. In "Aleluya", the final poem of the volume *Pregón de Marimorena*, Brindis de Salas presents a strong image of the black woman:

Piernas para caminar yo tengo que no se detendrán yo voy y vengo sin cesar. ¡Aleluya!	I have legs with which to walk; they will not falter. I go everywhere without hesitation. Hallelujah!

¡ALELUYA!

Virginia Brindis de Salas

Coro redentor que clamas
desde las Antillas
hasta el Plata
y en el río como mar
exclama:
 ¡Aleluya!

Pueblo americano
que soy tuya,
nací por ti
pues por ti voy
y digo así:
 ¡Aleluya!

Que de gente
hay en la calle,
y no hay nadie
que silencio
guarde.
 ¡Aleluya!

Son muchos
los que van a trabajar
y muchos son también
los que apenas comen
y quisieran cantar:
 ¡Aleluya!

Piernas
para caminar yo tengo
que no se detendrán
yo voy y vengo
sin cesar.
 ¡Aleluya!

HALLELUJAH!

Virginia Brindis de Salas

    Redeeming chorus shouting
    from the Antilles
    to the Plate River
    and in the sea-like river
    exclaims:
        Hallelujah!

    People of America,
    I am yours.
    I was born in you;
    because of you I exist
    and so I say:
        Hallelujah!

    So many people
    are there in the street
    and there is no one
    who maintains
    silence:
        Hallelujah!

    Many are those
    who are going to work
    and there are also many
    who hardly eat
    but yet would wish to sing:
        Hallelujah!

    I have legs
    with which to walk;
    they will not falter.
    I go everywhere
    without hesitation.
        Hallelujah!

Yo negra,
tú blanca mujer americana:
la misma sopa
habremos de comer
durante días y semanas;
lo mismo tú, mujer
de Europa,
has de comer igual que yo
la misma sopa,
y tendrás la misma fe
y la misma ropa
y has de beber tu vino
en igual copa.
    ¡Aleluya!

Que de gente
habrá en las calles
cuando salgan a batir
los parches de los pechos
por el aire.
    ¡Aleluya!

I, a black woman,
you, a white American woman:
the same soup
we must both eat
for days and weeks;
even you, woman
of Europe,
have to eat, the same as I
the same soup
and you probably have the same faith
and the same clothes
and you have to drink your wine
from the same cup:
    Hallelujah!

So many people
will be in the streets
whenever you go out:
    Hallelujah!

SEMBLANZA

Virginia Brindis de Salas

¿De dónde provienes tú
apasionada, exaltada?
Tu sangre vio los ardores
de la Nigeria espectante.
Combada
y de ébano arrogante
el mapa de tu mirada.
Tus axilas aromadas
vegetación de la selva.
Paso de la culebra
tus caderas,
muchacha negra.

PORTRAIT

Virginia Brindis de Salas

      Where do you come from,
      passionate and exalted one?
      Your blood saw the ardors
      of expectant Nigeria.
      Curved
      and arrogant like the ebony
      contour of your face.
      Your fragrant armpits
      like the flora of the jungle.
      Like the undulation of the snake
      your hips,
      black girl.

MADRIGAL

Virginia Brindis de Salas

      Tú miras mi carne morena
      con ojos que son dos ascuas;
      quisiera ser una fuente
      donde escancies sed de ansias.

      Quiero quemar la sangre
      de mis venas en el trópico
      de tu frenesí trashumante.

MADRIGAL

Virginia Brindis de Salas

> You look at my dark skin
> with your eyes like two hot coals;
> I would like to be a fountain
> where you quench your ardent desire.
>
> I want to warm the blood
> of my veins in the heat
> of your nomadic frenzy.

LA CONGA

Virginia Brindis de Salas

Tamborilero bate,
bate la lonja, lonjá.

Deja correr el rio
que se desagua en tu frente.

Dale negra, dale ya
que es la conga del solar.

Tamborilero bate,
bate la lonja, lonjá.

Mira que hermosa figura
hace la niña al danzar:
su cabellera teñida
parece espuma en el mar.

De ese memeo
de su mareo
un marinero
en un temporal.

¡Jesús, María, barbaridad!
Pollera,
enagua,
agita en el aire
el remolino de su danzar.

Rubia la niña
pálida y gracil
como una vela
de catedral.
Como la llama
rutila en vano,

THE CONGA

Virginia Brindis de Salas

Drummer, beat,
beat the drum, drum.

Let it run,
the river which springs on your forehead.

On with it, *negra*,
On with the ancestral conga.

Drummer, beat,
beat the drum, drum.

Look what a pretty figure
the dancing girl makes:
her tinted hair like
foam on the sea.

From the whirl
of her dizzyness,
a seafarer
in a storm.

My goodness, how amazing!
Wide skirt,
petticoat,
moving in the breeze
the whirl of her dancing.

A blond girl
pale and slender
as a candle
from the cathedral.
How the flame
flickers in vain,

¡Cristo!,
sus manos
quieren hundirse
por todo el aire
buscando el fuego
que a ella le quema
pies, sangre y venas;
y su cabeza
ya trastornada
gira y más gira
toda embotada
en las sincopadas
de su danzar.

¡Mira qué cara
negra Manuela!

Mira qué cara
pone la niña
junto a la conga
y a los congueros;
los tamboreros
en ella dibujan
las contraciones,
sus expresiones,
que hacen sumisa
a esa "pobre niña"
girar danzando
como una noria
en el vendaval.

Negra Manuela,
mira a tu amita;
va doblegada
en un tumulto
de saxofones.
Está embriagada
como con jora
y adobada
está de canela,
jengibre
aroma de selva en flor.

Goodness!
her hands
try to plunge
through the breeze
in search of a fire
which will burn
her feet, blood and veins;
and her head,
confused now,
turns and turns again
dazed by
the syncopation
of her dancing.

Look at her face
Negra Manuela!

Look what a face
the girl makes,
charmed by the "conga"
and the "conga" players;
the drummers
design in her
convulsions
and their expressions
which force
that "poor little girl"
to dance, spinning
like a noria
in a sea breeze.

Negra Manuela,
look at your little friend;
as she yields
to the tumult
of saxophones.
She is drunk
as if on palm wine
and she's spiced
with cinnamon,
ginger,
aroma of the jungle in bloom.

Si hasta parece su cabellera
que al entrar era
rubia, sedeña
en croquiñol
estar teñida
en aros de humo
cuando conturba
todo su cuerpo;
sus prominencias sobresalientes
del pecho al vientre
que trecho a trecho
recorren libres:
estar el acecho
del duro diente
del apetito.

¡Negra Manuela,
mira la conga
cuando la niña
tu amita danza!

Toda deshecha
tira su carne
que a los costados
se balancea...

¡Mira la niña!

Quién no lo crea
oiga los parches
batir por ella
lejos del suelo
de la manigua.

Oiga los parches batir por ella.

¡Bah!, si supiera
en su forma ambigua
que ella de negra
quiere vestirse,
oler a grajo
y a noche ardiente;
toda sedienta
toda ferviente

Even her hair
which at first was
blond, silky
in croquignole curls
now turns the color
of smoke rings
when she moves
her whole body;
her conspicuous protrusions
from chest to belly
move freely:
lying in wait for
the sharp tooth
of desire.

Negra Manuela,
look at the drum
when your little
friend dances!

In disarray
her whole flesh
undulating
from side to side...

Look at the girl!

You will believe if you
listen to the drums
beat for her
far from the floor
of the jungle.

Listen to the drums beat for her.

Bah! if she only knew
in her ambiguous form
that she wants
to be clothed in black,
to smell of earth
and ardent nights;
completely desirous
completely fervent

junto a la conga
y a los congueros;
junto a la lonja
a los tamboreros;
toda inconsciente
toda resuelta.
¡Hasta la cara
se le da vuelta!

Con estridencia
da la trompeta
ritmo y cadencia.

Baila tu amita
negra Manuela.

Se van las luces
ya de la noche.

Ay, y la llevan
negra Manuela
hasta su casa:
en parigüela!

close to the drum
and the drummers;
near the drum-head
and the drummers;
entirely oblivious
entirely contented.
Even her face
has changed!

Stridently
the trumpet
lends rhythm and cadence.

Your little friend dances,
Negra Manuela.

Now the night lights
grow dim.

Ay, and they carry her,
Negra Manuela,
to her house
on a stretcher.

UNGUET

Virginia Brindis de Salas

Tu corazón
arrulla, como el caracol
la vida del mar,
el patio y el zaguán
de nuestra casa.

Unguet,
quién te viera pasar
como una vara de mimbre
en el tembladeral.

Niña mi niña
recental de viejos seres
nacidos en la manigna.

Cuando tú puedas contar
lo que tus ojos vieron:
cuando tú puedas cantar
lo que tus oídos oyeron,
como el caracol
el susurro del mar.

Qué lejano mar,
para tu inquietante andar
Unguet,
como una vara de mimbre
hija del viento
en el tembladeral.

Y que tú puedas decir
Benguela o Mozambique
sin tener que maldecir
el barco que se va a pique.

UNGUET

Virginia Brindis de Salas

>Your heart
>courts the patio and foyer
>of our house,
>like the snail desires
>the life of the sea.
>
>Unguet,
>whoever sees you pass by
>like a willow frond
>in a quagmire.
>
>Child, my young
>child, product of the old ones
>born in the jungle.
>
>When you are able to tell
>what your eyes have seen:
>when you can sing the song
>that your ears have heard,
>like the snail reveals
>the secrets of the sea.
>
>What a distant sea,
>for your troubled voyage
>Unguet,
>like a willow frond
>child of the wind
>in the swamp.
>
>So that you may speak
>of Benguela or Mozambique
>without needing to curse
>the ship that founders.

Unguet,
hija sureña;
en el invierno
frio,
en el verano,
estío.

La vena tropical
de bisabuelo
seca y ancestral.
Este es tu suelo.

Unguet, daughter of the South;
in the winter
cold,
in the summer, warm.

The dry and ancestral
tropical fount
of our forbears.
This is your land.

PREGÓN NÚMERO UNO

Virginia Brindis de Salas

Toma mi verso
Marimorena
yo sé que los has de beber
como una copa de alcohol,
a cambio de él
quiero tu angustia
Marimorena.

Quiero tu angustia,
quiero tu pena,
toda tu pena
y el tajo de tu boca
cuando ríes
como una loca
Marimorena,
toda ebria
más que de vino,
de miseria.

Tu voz,
que nunca arrulló
a tus hijos
ni a tus nietos
y es voz de paria
arrulla mimosamente
toda la prensa diaria.

Y no hay quien te haga callar
por dos vintenes un diario
no hay quien deje de comprar
para aliviar tu sudario.

PREGÓN NUMBER ONE

Virginia Brindis de Salas

    Take my verses
    Marimorena.
    I know that you have to drink them
    like a shot of rum,
    but as a fair exchange
    I want your anguish,
    Marimorena.

    I want your anguish,
    I want your suffering,
    all of your suffering
    and the tilt of your mouth
    when you laugh
    like a crazy woman,
    Marimorena,
    drunk
    not so much on wine
    as on misery.

    Your voice,
    never singing lullabies
    to your children
    or grandchildren,
    a pariah's voice
    gently proffers
    the daily newspaper.

    There is no one to quiet you
    for four cents a paper;
    no one can refuse to buy one
    so as to lighten your burden.

Déjame ver tu cara
Marimorena,
que la atención acapara
causando lástima y pena.

Cuánto te deben
Marimorena,
esos que escriben
y que tú pagas
con tus vintenes,
con tus pregones,
por la mañana
y por la tarde
miles de veces;
en cambio tú
pagas con creces;
su periodismo
su propaganda politiquera
todas sus lacras, su egoísmo,
sus fementidas torpes carreras.

Marimorena
todos los días vende los diarios;
tiene una pena
Marimorena
y es su sudario.

Let me see your face
Marimorena,
for its expression captivates,
causing sorrow and pity.

They owe you so much,
Marimorena,
the ones who write
and whom you pay
with your pennies,
with your sales pitch,
in the morning
and in the afternoon
thousands of times;
on the other hand you
pay dearly for
their journalism,
their political propaganda
all their defects, their selfishness,
their false and dull careers.

Marimorena
sells newspapers every day;
Marimorena
suffers every day
her burden.

PREGÓN NÚMERO DOS

Virginia Brindis de Salas

A las seis de la mañana
por las calles de la ciudad
gira una voz por el aire;
pregón de Marimorena.

¿Qué noticias, qué noticias
del mundo trae la prensa?

A las cinco de la tarde;
pregón de Marimorena
como campana sonora
de los barrios populares;
pregón de Marimorena!

¿Quién te dió morena vieja
esa hermosa gritería
que sale de tus pulmones
agitando noche y dia
del mundo las sensaciones?

Pregonera de esperanzas
con los diarios bajo el brazo;
dos vintenes y una chanza
que tú olvidas calle abajo.

La noche de los suburbios
en tu mente es rediviva;
danzan corazones turbios
para que otros vivan.

¿Qué saben los "redactores"
como se vende un diario,
politicos o "doctores"
después del abecedario?

PREGÓN NUMBER TWO

Virginia Brindis de Salas

>At six in the morning
>through the streets of the city
>a voice rings in the air;
>the cry of the vendor, Marimorena.
>
>What news, what news
>of the world does the newspaper bring?
>
>At five in the afternoon;
>the call of Marimorena
>like a loud bell
>in the popular neighborhoods;
>the call of Marimorena!
>
>Old colored woman, who gave you
>that strident melody
>that comes from your lungs,
>proclaiming night and day
>the dramas of the world?
>
>Peddler of hopes
>with newspapers under your arm;
>four cents and small talk
>which you forget down the block.
>
>Nights in the suburbs
>come back to your mind;
>troubled hearts spin
>so that others may live.
>
>What do the editors know about
>how to sell a newspaper,
>or politicians or professors
>beyond their primer?

Tú, negra analfabeta,
Marimorena,
dia a dia, jeta a jeta,
las calles llenas
con pregones sandungueros:
en la mañana primero
y por la tarde después
durante los treinta dias
o trienta y uno del mes.

No hay sol que arredre nunca,
ni lluvia que te aglutine,
y si se empapa tu nuca
o chapotean tus botines,
vas adelante y pregonando
como heraldo en los mitines
y es un concierto tu anuncio
de todos los diarios juntos.

Cuando un señor de la prensa
pase a tu lado y te oiga
que no se escape de esta
y tus pregones desoiga:
para cuando tú no puedas
gritar el diario que escribe
pues sin el pan te quedas
y a ti nadie se suscribe.

Dile que en las columnas
del diario que ellos fabrican
pueden reclamar sin duda
jubilación para el canillita.

Pues pan para el que trabaja
y que trabajó en su vida
y que bregue por la caja
en la cámara en seguida;
y que siempre lo recuerde
que pioneros de la industria
—la industria del periodismo—
son todos los pregoneros
que como tú hacen lo mismo.

You, black illiterate woman,
Marimorena,
day to day, face to face
you fill the streets
with provocative sounds:
first in the morning
then in the afternoon
for thirty or thirty-one
days of each month.

No amount of sun keeps you away,
nor does the rain drive you back;
and if you get sopping wet
or your boots get soaked,
you keep right on peddling
like a herald at a rally
and you even make the names of your
papers flow like music from your lips.

When a man of the press
passes by you, and hearing your voice,
from which no one escapes,
yet he pretends not to hear:
so that when you can no longer
peddle the paper which he writes
you will be without a crumb,
and no one will subscribe to you.

Tell him that in the columns
of the newspaper that they produce
they can certainly announce
the retirement of the street vendor.
Let there be bread for the one who works
and has worked in her lifetime
and who struggles to make quick money
for the papers;
and tell him to remember always
that the pioneers of the industry
—the newspaper industry—
are all hawkers
who do the same things you do.

Oigan políticos,
periodistas,
que aquí hacen gordas sus vistas;
pues miren como ha vivido
Marimorena,
señores tan egoístas,
que nada nunca les ha pedido.

Pregón, tu pregón pregonera
de toda la prensa diaria,
Marimorena, morena
de mirada estrafalaria.
Tú haces más que las rotativas
y más que los linotipos
que cantan en los talleres.

¿Qué harían tantos obreros
si su labor no vendieras?
¿Qué harían con el tiraje
sin tu pregón solidario?
Administradores y empleados
y otros cómodos sentados?
. . . .
Por dos vintenes un diario,
Marimorena,
camino de su sudario.

Listen politicians,
journalists
who pretend not to see;
look you selfish gentlemen
how Marimorena, who has never
asked you for anything,
has lived.

Sound your pitch, saleswoman
of the daily press,
brown-skinned Marimorena
with your strange look.
You do more than the printing presses
and more than the linotypes
which hum in the workrooms.

What would become of their news
without your sound support,
those administrators and clerks
and other sedentary workers?

For four cents a paper,
Marimorena,
the cloth of her shroud.

Gastón Figueira

The Afro-Uruguayan Gastón Figueira was born in Montevideo in 1905. He is considered one of the chief exponents of the genre of black poetry in Uruguayan and Brazilian literature. His works include *Dulces visiones* (Sweet Visions), *Baladas* (Ballads), *En el templo de la noche* (In the Temple of Darkness), *Luz que canta* (The Singing Light), *El alma de la rosa* (The Soul of the Rose), and Volume Five of the *Geografía poética de América* (The Poetic Geography of America), which was published in Buenos Aires in 1939 and contains many poems of Afro-Brazilian inspiration.

In addition to his poetic production, Figueira has produced at least one critical analysis of the Afro-Hispanic poets Nicolás Guillén and Manuel del Cabral, the essay "Dos poetas iberoamericanos de nuestro tiempo" (Two Ibero-American Poets of Our Times). Another contribution to Hispanic literary scholarship is his study "Juan Ramón Jiménez, poeta de lo inefable" (Juan Ramón Jiménez, Poet of the Inexpressible).

The poem presented here, "Quitandeira", derives from the poet's collection *Alba en la playa de los mil cocoteros* (Dawn on the Beach of a Thousand Coconut Trees), 1939, which was inspired by Figueira's intimate love and knowledge of the rich traditions of Afro-Brazilian folklore and culture. In the poem, he invokes childhood memories of the *quitandeira*, a popular figure in the Bahian landscape, the coastal region of Brazil, where many of the inhabitants are of African descent. The poet's pleasure in recalling the intimate details of his childhood association with the *quitandeira* and explicit wish and implicit need to relive this time when life was colorful, yet simple and sweet, suggest that life has lost some of its original goodness and sweetness.

By focusing on the quaintness of her dress, Figueira tries to present a superficial vision of this unnamed black woman and maintain a certain distance from his subject. And yet he succeeds in conveying a definite feeling of intimacy and permanence through insistent use of words that suggest circularity: hoop skirt, rings, necklace, round pink candies, and coconuts.

QUITANDEIRA

Gastón Figueira

    Negra quitandeira bahiana
que ofreces tus dulces
con una sonrisa lánguida.
Buena quitandeira bahiana,
quiero volver a ser niño
comiendo tus cocadas,
tus cocadas blancas,
tus cocadas negras,
¡tan ricas, tan buenas!
Quitandeira bahiana
con tus aros, tus anillos, tus collares,
tu falda de matices cantantes,
tu blusa ancha
de encajes adornada,
y un pañuelo de colores vivientes
anudado en la frente.
En un braserito
calientas tus bollos de mandioca,
mientras la tarde taciturna
va muriendo
con una sonrisa lánguida
como la de tu alma.
Dame tus cocadas,
buena quitandeira,
tus cocadas blancas,
tus cocadas negras.
Dame tus "pés de moleque",
dame esos dulces redondos, color de rosa,
llamados "bejinhos de moca".
En tu bandeja ofreces, quitandeira bahiana,
dulcísimos pedacitos de infancia.

CANDY VENDOR

Gastón Figueira

Black candy vendor of Bahia,
offering your sweets
with a languid smile.
Good candy vendor of Bahia,
I want to be a child again,
eating your coconut drops
your white candies,
your black candies,
so delicious, so good!
Candy vendor of Bahia
with your hooped skirts, rings, necklaces,
your skirt of vivid tones,
your flowing blouse
adorned with lace,
and a kerchief of dazzling colors
tied around your head.
On a little stove
you heat your cassava cakes,
while the taciturn afternoon
fades away
with a languid smile,
like the smile of your soul.
Give me your coconut drops,
good candy vendor,
your white candies,
your black candies.
Give me your sweets,
give me those round, pink candies,
called *bejinhos de moca*.
On your tray you offer, *quitandeira*,[4]
sweet morsels of my childhood.

Pilar E. Barrios

Pilar E. Barrios, Afro-Uruguayan poet, man of letters and active patron of the arts, wrote the following autobiographical sketch, which appeared first in *Antologia de la poesia negra americana* (Anthology of Black American Poetry) by Ildefonso Pereda Valdés in 1936, and subsequently in the prologue to *Piel negra* (Black Skin) prepared by the Uruguayan writer Alberto Britos.

"I was born in Garzón, the second district of the department of Rocha, on the 12th of October, 1889, where my parents resided. Six months later, they moved to an area which was then known as Villa de San Carlos, second district of the department of Maldonado. They sent me to live with a family, which now resides in Montevideo, with the understanding that I be sent to school. My guardians kept their promise only in part because six months later, they withdrew me from school. I still remember part of the text of the letter which they sent (by me) to the school mistress. The letter was unsealed and written quite legibly, so that on the way to school, I read it spelling out the words and crying along the way. Among other things, the letter said: 'Furthermore, madam, the little black boy has learned enough, especially since he is not going to study to become a doctor.'

"Around 1900, they sent me to a place in the country called 'El Sauce', in the department of Lavalleja. Later they brought me home and out of necessity, since my father was no longer alive, they made me enroll in a public school.

"Readjusting to country life, I devoted myself to the healthy and simple existence of a country dweller. There I was taken by surprise by the revolution of 1904, having remained on the ranch for several months, in the company of another boy, since the boss had gone off to war with all of the peons. In 1907 there was a great change in the establishment. I took advantage of the change in order to sell some ranch animals which I owned. Then I packed up and left for (the department of) Minas. In October of the same year I entered the employ of Dr. Ernesto Seijo, at his villa near San Carlos, which was called 'El Peñasco'. There I composed various kinds of poetry, which I used to sing accompanied by the guitar, but I never wrote them down. It was in 1908 that I dedicated some *décimas* entitled 'Mi madre' to my mother.[5]

"My first poetry was published in 'El Civismo' in San Carlos, with the title 'A la Agraciada' [To the Graceful Woman]. By 1917, my sister Maria

Esperanza and my brother Ventura Barrios had founded the journal 'Nuestra Raza' [Our Race], and I published in it 'Noches de Amor' [Nights of Love], 'La Tricolor' [The Tricolored Flag], 'Mis cuitas' [My Cares] and other poems. Presently, I collaborate in the publication of 'Nuestra Raza', the journal."

The poems of Pilar Barrios were published in three volumes: *Piel negra* (Black Skin), which appeared in late 1947, *Mis cantos* (My Songs), published in 1949, and *Campo afuera* (Distant Fields), 1959, a collection of some forty poems which constitute a tribute to the Uruguayan gaucho.

The acclaim which the publication of *Piel negra* occasioned is documented in a number of letters and newspaper articles which were collected and published under the heading "Juicios y comentarios sobre el primer libro de Pilar E. Barrios, *Piel Negra*" (Opinions and Commentary on the First Book of Pilar E. Barrios, *Black Skin*) in his second volume of verse, *Mis cantos*. Friends and critics of *Piel Negra* included many members of the North, Central and South American intellectual and literary communities such as Langston Hughes, Juana de Ibarbourou, Ildefonso Pereda Valdés, Cristina Hernández de Gómez, and others.

In Pilar Barrios' poetry, the black woman, especially the black mother, receives much attention. His poem "Poema de la madre" (Poem for Mother), a fragment of which is included in this anthology, lavishes the mother with praise and appreciation. Barrios portrays her as:

lo más noble y más excelso	the noblest, the loftiest
es la creación más grande de Natura;	Nature's finest creation; and
y aunque no toda madre sabe serlo,	though not all know how to play the part,
la vida de la madre es un poema.	a mother's life is a poem.

POEMA DE LA MADRE

(Mi Respuesta)

Pilar E. Barrios

¿Influye en algo el color de la epidermis?
NO; una mujer, cualquiera sea su raza
desde que llega a la edad puberta,
es una madre en ciernas,
antesala por cuya abierta puerta
llegará un dia el engendro;
y ya, desde ese instante,
vive, sigue y pasa,
la misma evolución, e igual proceso
hasta que en el momento culminante,
sentirá el natural desgarramiento,
tanto que esa madre sea una reina,
como que a una tribu pertenezca,
que sea de sangre azul o sea plebeya,
que tenga la piel blanca o la piel negra.

Hay sí, un serio problema
que altera y ensombrece el panorama
y está sin solución hasta el presente;
y es que la madre negra
sufre el doble prejuicio; el del pigmento
y el de ser indigente.
Pero... ¿no es ese mismo drama
cruel, terrible y sangriento
que vive, sufre y siente
todo el desheredado de la tierra?
. . . .
La madre es lo más noble y más excelso
es la creación más grande de Natura;
y aunque no toda madre sabe serlo,
la vida de la madre es un poema,
compendio de amor, lealtad y de ternura,
la madre es un cristal que el dolor quiebra
cuya amplitud no tiene paralelo,
la madre es, la realidad más pura
¡no excluye esa virtud a la madre negra!

MOTHERS

(My Response)

Pilar E. Barrios

Does the color of the skin somehow matter?
NO; a woman, whatever her race,
from the time she attains the age of puberty,
is a mother-in-waiting,
a foyer through whose open door
a child will one day appear;
and then she continues and goes through
the same evolution, an identical process
until at the final moment
she will feel a natural rending,
whether she be a queen,
or whether she belong to a tribe,
whether she be royalty or common,
whether her skin be white or black.

There is, however, a serious question
which changes and clouds the situation
and for which there is no solution;
and it is that a black mother
suffers from a double prejudice; of color
and of being indigent.
But . . . is it not the same cruel,
terrible and bloody drama
which is shared, suffered and felt
by all the exiled of the earth?
. . . .
A mother is the noblest and loftiest
she is Nature's finest creation;
and although not all know how to play the part,
a mother's life is a poem,
a compendium of love, loyalty and tenderness;
a mother is a crystal which pain shatters
and whose fullness is without equal,
a mother is the purest reality.
Do not exclude that virtue from a black mother!

¡NEGRA!

Pilar E. Barrios

A mi me dijeron negra
¡Dios mío! ¡Cuánto me reí!
Porque quien me lo dijera,
no era más que un infeliz.

Uno de esos seres fatuos
que se encuentran por doquier,
que no saben, que no saben,
pero que creen saber.

Y adoptan poses y gestos
de persona superior;
y hablan con empaque austero
para impresionar mejor,

y van haciendo un desfile
de genios al por mayor,
para hacer ver que son dueños
de una gran erudición...

Y asi nos hablan de Homero,
de Confucio o Cicerón,
e ignoran de aquí, a Zorrilla,
a Herrera y Reissig y a Rodó.

Tal el señor que con énfasis,
petulancia y rigidez,
me señalara con mofa
la negrura de mi ser.

¿Acaso soy yo culpable
o debo sentir vergüenza,
por el color que me dió
la Madre Naturaleza?

BLACK WOMAN

Pilar E. Barrios

They called me black woman
My Goodness! How I laughed!
Because the one who said that to me,
was no more than a wretch.

One of those fatuous persons
who are to be found everywhere,
who know nothing at all,
but who think they know everything.

And they assume postures and poses
of a superior person;
and they speak in an austere manner
in order to create a better impression,

and they surround themselves
with wholesale geniuses,
to make it seem that they are possessors
of great erudition . . .

And they speak to us about Homer,
about Confucius or Cicero,
and yet they know nothing of Zorrilla,
Herrera y Reissig or Rodó.

Such was the gentleman who, with emphasis,
petulance and rigidity
would point out to me mockingly
the blackness of my being.

Am I perhaps guilty
or should I feel ashamed
of the color given to me
by Mother Nature?

Si es la vida un accidente,
como el nacer y el morir
y en el correr de la vida,
puede el pigmento influir.

Hay mil distintos factores
que deben intervenir;
y eso, a un blanco, como a un negro,
igual le puede ocurrir.

Natural, que una piel blanca,
tersa y aterciopelada,
aunque no llene el espíritu,
llena siempre la mirada.

Y aún más, a quien lo deslumbra
el brillo de lo exterior,
por que no ve las tinieblas
ocultos en lo interior...

El medio, la inteligencia,
el régimen que vivimos,
el grado de ilustración
e instrucción que recibimos

son las únicas causales
y por ende el gran factor,
lo demás... son derivados
de la linea de color...

En la mujer blanca o rubia
¿Qué hay de superior a mí?
Si reuno las cualidades
que acabo de referir.

Somos hermanas gemelas
en el placer y en el sufrir
afines en sentimientos,
en el pensar y en el sentir.

De iguales inclinaciones
en nuestra virginidad,
de instintos nobles o crueles
en nuestra maternidad.

If life is another accident
like being born and dying
then in the course of life,
can skin color really matter?

There are a thousand different things
that should be considered;
which could happen as easily
to a white as to a black.

Of course, a white skin
smooth and velvety
although it doesn't satisfy the soul,
always attracts attention.

And for those who are dazzled
by the luster of the exterior,
why don't they see the dark
shadows of the interior?

The manner, the intelligence,
the regimen by which we live,
the level of erudition
and learning which we receive

are the real determinants
and therefore the prime factors,
the rest . . . is derived
from the color line . . .

What is there in the white woman or blonde
which is superior to me?
If I possess all the qualities
which I have just mentioned.

We are twin sisters
in pleasure and in suffering,
akin in emotions,
in thought and in feelings.

Of the same inclinations
in our virginity,
of the same noble or base instincts
in our maternity.

Sólo no somos iguales
en el aspecto social,
porque a ello, se interpone
la hipócrita sociedad.

Except that we are not equal
in the social sense,
because upon this is imposed
a hypocritical society.

Notes

[1] Jackson, *Black Writers*, pp. 93-94.
[2] Julio Guadalupe, "Prólogo: Virginia Brindis de Salas y su poesía realista", in Virginia Brindis de Salas, *Pregón de Marimorena* (Montevideo: Sociedad Cultural Editorial Indoamericana, 1946), p. 9. "Decía más adelante que Virginia B. de Salas desandó el camino emprendido por casi la mayoría de las mujeres poetas que bebieron en la fuente de las románticas sentimentales que las precedieron."
[3] Jackson, *The Black Image*, p. 99.
[4] "quitandeira", Portuguese spelling of the Spanish word "quitandera" which refers to a woman who was a member of a group of prostitutes who practiced their profession in a tent and who moved from one site to another. In addition to the prostitution activities, the "Quitandera" was a vendor of food and drink.
[5] Pilar E. Barrios, *Piel negra* (Montevideo: Nuestra Raza, 1947; rpt. Kraus-Thomson, 1970, n.pag.) "Nací en Garzón, 2a Sección del Departamento de Rocha, el 12 de Octubre de 1889, donde residían mis padres, quienes seis años después se radicaban en la entonces Villa de San Carlos, 2a Sección del Departamento de Maldonado. Allí me colocaron con una familia que hoy vive en Montevideo, con el compromiso de que me mandaran al colegio, cosa que hicieron a medias, por cuanto a los seis meses de haberme puesto allí me retiraron. Aún recuerdo parte del texto de la carta que le dirigían a la maestra y que por ir abierta y con letra muy clara, yo fui leyendo, deletrando y llorando durante el trayecto. Decía así, después de otras cosas: 'por lo demás, señorita, el negrito ya sabe bastante, y además no va a estudiar para doctor.'

"Por el año 1900 me mandaron a un establecimiento de campo en un lugar denominado 'El Sauce', Departamento de Lavalleja. Luego me trajeron y a instancias—mi padre no existía ya—me hicieron ingresar en una escuela pública.

"Reintegrado de nuevo al campo, me dediqué a la vida sana y sencilla del campesino. Allí me sorprendió la revolución de 1904, habiendo quedado en la estancia en compañía de otro chico por varios meses, por haberse marchado a la guerra el patrón con todos los peones. Corría el año 1907 y hubo un gran cambio en el establecimiento, que yo aproveché para reducir a dinero algunos animales que tenía y liando mis petates salí rumbo a Minas. En octubre del mismo año entré al servicio del Dr. Ernesto Seijo, en su casa-quinta cerca de San Carlos, denominada 'El Peñasco'. Allí compuse algunos versos de distinta índole, que cantaba en la guitarra y que nunca escribí. Fue por el año 1908 cuando le dediqué a mi madre unas décimas tituladas 'Madre mía'."

VENEZUELA

Andrés Eloy Blanco　　　　"Píntame Angelitos Negros"

Manuel Rodríguez-Cárdenas　"Apunte Para un 'Close-Up' de Eusebia Cosme"
"Canción de la Negra Juana"
"El Merengue Final"
"Tu Risa"
"La Canción de la Negrita"

Miguel Otero Silva　　　　"La Infancia"

Andrés Eloy Blanco

Andrés Eloy Blanco devoted his life to politics and literature. This Venezuelan statesman and man of letters was born in the province of Cumana on August 6, 1897. As a child, he experienced a loss of personal freedom as a result of his family's anti-government sentiments, an experience which repeated itself throughout his life, being alternately in and out of favor with the existing government. At one point, he was even incarcerated for his political activities.

He received a law degree from the Universidad Central in 1920. However, his recognition as a talented poet came earlier, in 1913, when his first poems were published, at age 16. Several years later, in 1918, he published his collection of poems *Canto a la espiga y el arado* (Hymn to the Tassle and the Plow) and his verse play *El huerto de la epopeya* (The Garden of the Epic). Other poetic works include *Tierras que me oyeron* (Lands Which Understood Me), 1921, and *Canto a España* (Hymn to Spain), 1923, for which he won the prize in an international competition sponsored by the Real Academia Española (Royal Spanish Academy). He later published *Poda* (Pruning Season), 1934, a collection of poems composed between 1923 and 1928; *Barco de piedras* (Stone Ship), 1937, and *Baedeker 2,000*, 1938. After the belated publication of the latter volume, Blanco made the following announcement:

> I have given up the poet's life. This does not mean that I will not continue to write poetry. I am always writing poems; I write them constantly; but always in the hours when politics allows me a respite ... I entered the political battle at a very early age, forced by reality. Sometimes I wanted to return completely to literature; but if I had decided to do so, perhaps I would not have been able to; it is not that the multitudes seek me as a political leader; it is rather that as long as there are a hundred men and a hundred women who ask me not to abandon an arena where my words could be useful, I would not have the right to deny them. Politics obligates the same as art.[1]

Giving up poetry was a real sacrifice, for being a poet was second nature to him, as he explains in the following passage:

> More than a politician, I am a man of letters; a man whom Politics has borrowed from Poetry, in the name of the responsibility of thought. If I represent anything in the struggle it is as an insurgent who is opposed to the olympic isolation of the artist, isolation from social concerns, from contact with the earth and its beings; a consciousness of the human debt

which has constructive work for all of mankind running the gamut from poet to mason...[2]

The poetic voice of Andrés Blanco was silent for some thirteen years until the appearance of *A un año de tu luz* (On Your First Birthday) in 1951. In 1954, he published the volume *Giraluna* (Moonflower). His last published collection of poetry, *Canto a los hijos* (Hymn to the Children), appeared in 1955, the year of his death in Mexico City.

"Andrés Eloy Blanco was and is the most popular of the Venezuelan poets, a reputation which he earned not only for his outstanding participation in his nation's public life, not only for his fine contribution as a poet, but for having captured, more than anyone, the soul of the people of Venezuela and their traditions."[3] His poem "Pintame angelitos negros" (Paint Me Some Black Angels) has appeared in almost every anthology of Afro-Hispanic poetry, enjoying popularity in Latin America and Europe. One of the most popular and talented Afro-North American singer-musicians, Roberta Flack, recorded the poem on her album *Take One*.

Blanco produced a variety of poetry, much of which was inspired by black culture. His poem "Pintame angelitos negros" expresses the injustice that has been suffered by blacks in Venezuela and in America, an injustice which extends even to the idea of a heaven made for whites only.[4] Although the black theme is not a major element in the poetry of this white Venezuelan poet, this poem "Pintame angelitos negros" is perhaps his best known work.

PÍNTAME ANGELITOS NEGROS

Andrés Eloy Blanco

¡Ah, mundo..., la negra Juana
la mala que le pasó!
¿Se le murió su negrito?
Si señó. Ah, compadrito del alma,
lo sano que estaba el negro.
Yo no le miraba el pliegue,
yo no le acataba el güeso;
como yo me enflaquecia
lo media con mi cuerpo.
Se me iba poniendo flaco
como yo me iba poniendo.

    "Ya se murió mi negrito,
    Dios lo tenía dispuesto.
    Ya lo tendrá colocao
    como angelito del cielo."
    Desengáñese, comae,
    si no hay angelitos negros.

Pintor de santos de alcoba,
pintor sin tierra en el pecho,
que cuando pintas tus santos
no te acuerdas de tu pueblo.
Y cuando pintas tus virgenes
pintas angelitos bellos,
pero nunca te acordaste
de pintar un ángel negro.

    Pintor nacido en mi tierra
    con el pincel extranjero,
    pintor que sigues el rumbo
    de tantos pintores viejos,
    aunque la Virgen sea blanca,
    píntame angelitos negros.

PAINT ME SOME BLACK ANGELS

Andrés Eloy Blanco

Oh Lord . . . , the troubles that
the black Jane has seen!
Did her little boy die?
Yes, sir. Ah, my dear friend,
her little boy seemed so healthy
I did not notice his flabbiness,
I paid no attention to his boniness;
since I was getting thin myself
naturally, I compared him to me.
He was getting thin
the same as I was.

> "My little black boy has died,
> It was God's will.
> He probably already has him
> as one of his heavenly angels."
> Don't kid yourself, my friend,
> there are no black angels.

Painter of saints for bedroom walls,
who bears no love for his people,
so when you paint your saints
you forget your own people.
And when you paint your virgins
you paint beautiful little angels,
but you never remember
to paint a black angel.

> Painter born in my land
> with a foreign brush in your hand,
> painter who follows the lead
> of so many old painters,
> even if you paint the Virgin white,
> paint me some black angels.

No hubo pintor que pintara
angelitos de mi pueblo,
ángel de buena familia,
no basta para mi cielo.
Yo quiero angelitos rubios
con angelitos trigueños.
Aunque la Virgen sea blanca,
píntame angelitos negros.

Si queda un pintor de santos,
si queda un pintor de cielos,
que haga el cielo de mi tierra
con los tonos de mi pueblo;
con sus ángeles catires,
con sus ángeles trigueños;
con sus angelitos blancos,
con sus angelitos negros;
con su ángel de perla fina,
con su ángel de medio pelo,
que vayan comiendo mangos
por las barriadas del cielo.

>   Igual que pintas tu tierra
>   así has de pintar tu cielo,
>   con un sol que tuesta blancos,
>   con un sol que tuesta negros,
>   porque para eso lo tienes
>   calentito y de los buenos.
>   Aunque la Virgen sea blanca,
>   píntame angelitos negros.

Si al cielo voy algún día
he de hallarte allá en el cielo,
angelitico del diablo,
serafín cucurucero.
No hubo una iglesia de rumbo,
no hay una iglesia de pueblo
donde hayan dejado entrar
el cuadro: "Angelitos negros."
Y entonces, ¿a dónde van
angelitos de mi pueblo,
zumuritos de Guaviare,
torditos de Barlovento?

Not a single painter would paint
little angels from among my people,
a middle class angel
will not suffice for my heaven.
I want little blond angels
along with dark-haired angels.
Although the Virgin be white,
paint little black angels for me.

If a painter of saints remains,
if there's still a painter of skies,
let him color the heaven of my land
with the hues of my people;
with its blond angels,
with its dark-haired angels;
with its little white angels,
with its little black angels,
with its little rich angels,
with its little poor angels,
running around heaven
eating mangoes.

> You must paint your heaven
> with the colors of your land,
> with a sun that tans whites,
> with a sun that tans blacks,
> that's why you have
> such a selection.
> Even if the Virgin is white
> paint me some little black angels.

If I get to heaven some day
I am certain to find you there,
my little devil,
my little angel.
There was no high-class church,
there is no ordinary church
where the picture "Black Angels"
is permitted to hang.
So tell me, where do the little
angels from my town go,
those black kids from Guaviare,
those black kids from Barlovento?

Si quieres pintar tu cielo
igual que pintas tu tierra,
cuando pintes angelitos
acuérdate de tu pueblo,
y al lado del ángel blanco
y junto al ángel trigueño,
aunque la Virgen sea blanca,
píntame angelitos negros.

If you want to paint your sky
the same as you paint your land,
when you paint little angels
remember your own people,
and alongside the white angel
and next to the brunette angel,
even though the Virgin is white,
paint me some little black angels.

Manuel Rodríguez-Cárdenas

The "copper-colored" Venezuelan poet, born in the state of Yaracay in 1912, Manuel Rodriguez-Cárdenas manifests in his work the deep impression made on him by the folklore of the black population in Venezuela.[5] His first published volume of poetry, *Tambor, poemas para los negros y mulatos* (Drum: Poems for Blacks and Mulattos), appeared in 1938.

The *autobiografismo*, which Stanley Cyrus suggests is an important element in Afro-Latin American literature,[6] and which Julián Padrón, prologuist of Rodriguez-Cárdenas' *Tambor*, views as a necessary and constant point of departure of all first works by an author, courses through the poems of Manuel Rodríguez-Cárdenas.[7]

The black women proffered by him assume a variety of guises: the sad merengue dancer, Juana, whose grace and charm give much pleasure to her admirers but who suffers a tragic destiny imposed by a society which devalues her black skin; Rosedá, another merengue dancer, who entrances the onlookers with the frenzied abandon of her dance movements:

El cuerpito retinto se tuerce y salta,	Her fragile black body twists and leaps,
se atornilla, se curva, se parte en dos;	turns, bends, and doubles over;
se agazapa con una saña felina...	arching with feline fury...

Still another black woman, past her prime and too old to dance the merengue, dreams of her youth:

soñando en sus tiempos	daydreaming of yer youth,
se menea, escondida	she dances, well-hidden
tras el panolón.	beneath her large shawl.

APUNTE PARA UN CLOSE-UP DE EUSEBIA COSME[8]

Manuel Rodríguez-Cárdenas

>   Salud,
>   graciosa mujer
>   que al Tambo
>   del Timbo llevas
>   la plenitud.
>   Africa Santa
>   ruge en tu boca
>   con mil tambores
>   de Tombuctú.

NOTES ON A CLOSE-UP OF EUSEBIA COSME

Manuel Rodríguez-Cárdenas

>Greetings to you
>delightful woman
>who brings
>the treasure
>from the Timbo
>to the Tambo.
>Blessed Africa
>roars from your lips
>with a thousand drums
>from Timbuktu.

CANCIÓN DE LA NEGRA JUANA

Manuel Rodríguez-Cárdenas

Diástole y sístole negra,
carbón de espejos lucientes,
mudo sabor de coquitos
pescados sobre la arena,
Juana la negrita; Juana
breve, apretadita y dulce
como una definición.

Y hay en el barrio mujeres
hermosas y perros tristes,
cacharrería rubicunda
de casas escalonadas,
tres por cuatro de joropos
sabrosos a pan tostado;
hay una victrola turbia,
dos cipreses y un castaño
y una luna quinceañera
que cuelga como amarrada
de un poste de arrabal.

Hay de todo en estas calles
polvosas y cribiformes;
pero yo, el poeta triste,
solo le canto a la negra,
porque Juanita es el alma-
mater de mi barrio abstracto:
síntesis de los abuelos
de toda la vecindad.

Y hoy el barrio está de gala
porque Juana va a bailar.

Cintarajos de colores
sobre la frente se ha puesto;

SONG OF THE "NEGRA" JUANA

Manuel Rodríguez-Cárdenas

    Diastolic and systolic black girl,
bright shiny charcoal
unspoken flavor
of fish over the sand,
Juana the black girl; petite
Juana, compact and as pleasing
as a definition.

    And in the *barrio* there are pretty
women and sad dogs,
golden-red earth of
the houses with steps,
filling the air with the aroma
of *joropos* with toasted bread;
there's an old victrola,
two cypresses and a chestnut
and a fortnight moon
which hangs as if fastened
to a neighborhood lamp post.

    Everything is seen here on these
dusty and run-down streets;
but I, the sad poet,
sing only for the black girl,
because little Juana is the soul-
mother of my abstract ghetto:
synthesis of all the ancestors
of the neighborhood.

    And today everyone's excited
because Juana is going to dance.

    On her head she wears
colored ribbons;

en el pecho una magnolia
y un malabar y un clavel;
en labios triquitraques
del papel más colorado;
pintura sobre las uñas
de la que tira a morado;
y un caminar ha ensayado
tan rítmico y sandunguero,
que los pechitos le bailan
como dos jarros morenos
que se fueran a romper.

Todo el barrio está de gala
porque llegó el carnaval
y a las ventanas se asoma
por ver a Juana pasar.

—Mira, ¡qué negra!, Maneto.
—Piazo é mujer, Camaleón.
—Si no es un mismo muñeco,
será la Virgen del Cielo
que se ha tornado en carbón...

Y se escalonan los dichos
como lucientes reflejos
por donde pasa la negra.
Y se escalofrían los ojos
como pompas de jabón.
Y las intenciones son,
más que de agudos puñales,
de ardientes y agrios cristales
puestos a brillar al sol.

En tanto, muere la tarde
rumiando rubias tristezas,
y un farol y otro farol
se dan la tenue manita
para espolvorear cocuyos
entre el pelo de la noche
silente, del arrabal.

—Allá va la negra Juana,
mírala, vé como va:

on her breast a magnolia,
a malabar and a carnation;
on her lips confetti
of the reddest paper;
polish on her nails
of a purple color;
and she has learned a new walk
so rhythmic and elegant,
that her breasts bounce
like two brown jars
about to break.

The whole *barrio* is excited
because it's carnival time
and they go to the windows
to see Juana walk by.

—Look, what a black girl, Maneto.
—What a woman, Camaleón.
—If she's not a living doll,
she must be the Virgin Mary
who has turned herself black.

And the comments spread
about her path
like lightning.
And their eyes quiver
like soap bubbles.
And their intentions are,
more than of sharp daggers,
of ardent and acrid crystals
put out to glisten in the sun.

Meanwhile, the afternoon fades
reflecting on blond sorrows,
a light, then another light
join delicate hands
to sprinkle glowworms
on the hair of the
silent night, of the ghetto.

—Here comes the *negra* Juana,
look at her, see how she walks;

trenzando su risa negra,
blanca por casualidad.
—Negrita, ¿vas a la plaza?
—Si, negro, vamo a bailá.

Moviendo el cuerpo tinto
como quien bate café.
—Negrita, ¿vas a la plaza?
—Si, negro, vamo a bailá.

Al aire sus quince cintas
como un penacho de sol.
—Negrita, ¿vas a la plaza?
—Si, negro, vamo a bailá.

Las caderas ritmo prieto,
prieto olor el caminar.
—Negrita, vas a la plaza?
—Si, negro, vamo a bailá.

—Si, negro, vamo a bailá,
parece a todos decir!

Y cuando el joropo vibra
en la estremecida plaza;
cuando los cohetes peinan
sus caminos indecisos
entre la criolla fanfarria;
cuando el viento con insomnio
corcovea en caprichos niños
sobre los cuerpos urgidos,
se va Juana, entre los brazos
del más raudo bailarín.
Peces de sudor le brincan
sobre el jabonado seno.

La negra baila un merengue
y a más de bailar, parece
que se está deshilachando
sobre su cuerpo un torrente
de adormecida lascivia;
que su vida entera gira
sobre el tornillo sin fin
de las crujientes caderas;

flashing her black smile,
white by chance.
—*Negrita*, are you going to the square?
—Yes, *Negro*, let's dance.

Moving her black body
like someone grinding coffee.
—*Negrita*, are you going to the square?
—Yes, *Negro*, let's dance.

In the breeze, her fifteen ribbons
like a crest of light.
—*Negrita*, are you going to the square?
—Yes, *Negro*, let's dance.

Her hips, black rhythm,
black perfume, her walk.
—*Negrita*, are you going to the square?
—Yes, *Negro*, let's dance.

—Yes, *Negro*, let's dance,
she seems to say to all.

And when the *joropo* vibrates
in the animated square;
when the rockets design
their capricious path
over the creole fanfare;
when the restless wind
dances with childish glee
on the active bodies,
Juana appears, in the arms
of the ablest dancer.
Beads of sweat form
on her soap-scented breast.

The *Negra* dances a merengue
and while dancing, it seems
that over her body is unleashed
a torrent of dormant wantonness;
as if her whole being hinges
on the endless spinning
of her swaying hips;

que los piés menudos vuelan
entre un fragor de cantáridas.

Y aquel temblor de su vientre
poniendo oblicuos los ojos;
aquellas manos tendidas
como un puente de esquiveces
—mil veces sí, cien mil no—;
aquel mover de los muslos
con arrastrante lujuria;
aquella curva ondulante
que es su esqueleto de fuego
más que el palpitar de un ritmo
parecen—muerta candela—
todo el ardor de una tribu
sedienta sobre un tambor.

Casi da miedo mirar
cuando bailando va Juana.

A las tres, cuando su hamaca
hiló el gallo de luceros,
se apagaron las bombillas
tenues de la riente plaza.

La luna fingía un chinesco
farol muerto. La hojarasca
de papelillos caídos
se removía con la brisa...
y entre el brillo de ladrillo
más que amarillo—lunar—,
los árboles eran mudas
admiraciones de sombra.

Juana va por la empedrada
calle de mi abstracto barrio.
Va pensando en la menuda
pena de su vida lenta;
en la tristeza que tienen
los días iguales que vienen;
en la vida sin amores
que la espera, porque es negra
y las negras no conocen

as if her tiny feet fly
amidst the clamor of cantharides.

And that trembling of her belly
drawing oblique looks from the crowd;
her hands stretched out
like a scornful bridge
—a thousand times yes, a hundred thousand no—;
that movement of her thighs
with forlorn wantonness;
that wavy curve
of her fiery body
more than the beat of a rhythm
seems—a smouldering fire—
all the ardor of an eager tribe
on a drum.

It is almost frightening to watch
Juana when she dances.

At three o'clock, when the morning
rooster put up his hammock,
they put out the tenuous
lights of the laughing square.

The moon was like a dead
Chinese lantern. Abandoned
paper streamers
were tossed by the breeze...
And against the sheen of bricks
more than yellow—moonlit—,
the trees were silent
miracles of darkness.

Juana walks through the cobblestone
street of my abstract *barrio*.
Thinking about the frequent
hardships of her dull life;
of the sadness of the
monotonous days to come;
life without love
awaits her, because she is black
and black women cannot hope for

ni novios ni matrimonios.
—Ah malhaya, quién pudiera
ser blanca como la luna!

Y allí se ha quedado, quieta
junto al poste de la esquina,
mirando los dedos rosa
de la mañana que viene;
oteando el callado silbo
de los sauces llorones,
y así esta pena de raza
frente al castaño ha confiado:
—Ah malhaya, quién pudiera
ser blanca como la aurora!

Ah malhaya, quién pudiera!,
repite el viento. ¡Ah malhaya!
Quién a Juana conociera
de verla en esta mañana...

Tres días más tarde, moría
la rosa negra en el barrio:
unos dicen que de pena,
otros que de pulmonía.

Sólo Dios y el perro "Chancho"
el secreto conocían.
El castaño no lo dijo
porque el alma le dolía,
y los sauces lo callaron
porque no les convenía.

Hoy el arrabal bosteza
de fastidio con los sauces,
el castaño y las mujeres;
con el joropo amarrado
entre la turbia victrola
y la luna acatarrada
que se resfrió de luceros.

¡Qué triste estamos hoy todos!
Parece que nos dolieran

sweethearts or marriage.
—Ah, if only I were
as white as the moon!

And there she remained, quietly
leaning on the corner lamppost,
looking at her fingers, rose of
the approaching morning;
hearing the quiet sound
of the two weeping willows.
And she confided to the chestnut
this racial shame:
—Ah, if only I were
as white as the dawn!

Ah, poor soul, foolish wish!
the wind repeats. Poor soul!
Anyone who knew Juana
seeing her that morning...

Three days later, the black
rose of the *barrio* died:
some say of grief,
others say of pneumonia.

Only God and the dog Chancho
knew her secret.
The chestnut tree did not tell it
because its heart ached,
and the willows kept their silence
because it suited them.

Today the *barrio* yawns,
bored with the willows,
the chestnut tree and the women;
as well as the *joropo* rhythm
loudly playing on the victrola
and the callous moon
chilled by the morning stars.

How sad we all are now!
It seems that our eyes are suffering

los ojos de tanto vernos,
porque ni los niños gritan,
ni juegan las paraulatas
gárgaro rubio en los cables.

Nos está doliendo Juana,
la de cintura de fuego,
que se nos fué una mañana
por no haber nacido blanca.

Y es que Juana no sabía,
a fuerza de ser tan blanca,
que tenía la risa blanca
y el alma clara, muy clara.

En las ventanas como antes
nadie volverá a mirar,
ni el barrio estará de gala
cuando llegue el carnaval.

¿Por qué nos dejaste, Juana,
si te habíamos de llorar?

En tanto silencio corre
tejiendo locas consejas:
unos dicen que de pena,
otros que de pulmonía.

Mañana hablarán los viejos
como hilvanando el vacío:
—Cuando la negra se fué,
la causa nadie sabía:
el castaño no lo dijo
porque el alma dolía,
y los sauces lo callaron
porque no les convenía.

Sobre el aspa de los vientos,
gira la leyenda fría.
¡Sólo Dios y el perro "Chancho"
el secreto conocían!

from seeing so much of ourselves,
even the children don't shout any more,
and the cables don't vibrate
with their red gargle.

We are mourning for Juana,
the one with the fiery waist,
who left us one morning
for not being born white.

And Juana longed so to be white,
that she didn't seem to know,
that she had a white smile
and a very limpid soul.

Nobody will again look out
the window as before,
nor will the *barrio* get all dressed up
when it's carnival time again.

Why did you leave us, Juana,
to grieve and mourn for you?

While the silence moves along
weaving strange rumors:
some say from grief,
others from pneumonia.

Tomorrow the old people will talk,
trying to mend their loneliness:
—When the *Negra* went away,
no one knew the reason:
the chestnut did not tell
because its heart ached,
and the willows kept their silence
because it pleased them to do so.

On the wings of the wind,
spins the cruel legend.
Only God and the dog Chancho
knew her secret.

EL MERENGUE FINAL

Manuel Rodríguez-Cárdenas

    Dale, dale, dale, dale,
dale, dale, dale ya.
Dale, dale, dale, dale,
dale, dale, Rosedá.

    Moviendo la cintura con ritmo lento,
las dos manos tendidas, el vientre hirviendo,
surje en estos momentos entre la rueda
el cuerpo de guitarra de Rosedá.

    La falda de zaraza cruje y ondula
sobre sus pies bruñidos de celofán
y le brincan los senos entre el corpiño
de bordado y sedoso madapolán.

    Un negro que se curva sobre la mina
arranca del tarugo su rico són
y ensordecen el aire las zapatetas
tejidas entre el ritmo de las curvetas
y el llanto ronco y gordo del guitarrón.

    Dale, dale, dale, dale,
dale, dale, dale ya.
Dale, dale, dale, dale,
dale, dale, Rosedá.

    El cuerpito retinto se tuerce y salta,
se atornilla, se curva, se parte en dos;
se agazapa con una saña felina
y parece el escorzo de una pimpina
mecido entre los tumbos de la piñata
sobre un mar sandunguero de agua de arroz.

THE LAST MERENGUE

Manuel Rodríguez-Cárdenas

    Dale, dale, dale, dale,
dale, dale, dale ya
Dale, dale, dale, dale,
Dale, dale, Rosedá.[9]

    Moving her waist with a slow rhythm,
her hands outstretched, her belly on fire,
at that moment appears among the crowd
the guitar-shaped figure of Rosedá.

    Her chintz skirt rustles and ripples
around her glistening brown feet
and her breasts rise up from her corset
of silky embroidered percale.

    A Negro bends over his drum,
wrenching from the wood a rich sound
and the air is filled with his foot-patting
woven into the rhythm of the drums
and the sturdy, hoarse cry of the big guitar.

    Dale, dale, dale, dale,
dale, dale, dale ya
Dale, dale, dale, dale,
Dale, dale, Rosedá.

    Her frail black body twists and leaps,
turns, bends and doubles over;
she arches herself with feline fury
looking like a dwarfish jug
rocked among the ingredients of a pinata
on a graceful sea of rice water.

Dale, dale, dale, dale,
dale, dale, dale ya.
Dale, dale, dale, dale,
dale, dale, Rosedá.

Gira la cintura,
cruge la cadera,
zumban los bordones
en el guitarrón
y una negra vieja
soñando en sus tiempos
se menea, escondida
tras el pañolón.

Dale, dale, dale, dale,
dale, dale, dale ya.
Dale, dale, dale, dale,
dale, dale, Rosedá.

Dale, dale, dale, dale,
dale, dale, dale ya
Dale, dale, dale, dale,
Dale, dale, Roseda.

She whirls her waist,
shakes her hips,
the bass strings quiver
on the big guitar
and an old black woman
daydreaming of her youth
she dances, well-hidden
beneath her large shawl.

Dale, dale, dale, dale,
dale, dale, dale ya
Dale, dale, dale, dale,
Dale, dale, Roseda.

TU RISA

Manuel Rodríguez-Cárdenas

    Te envidiaría una mazorca
tus dientes de maíz pilado
cuando te ríes por los goces,
negra, que te da mi mano.

    Yo no sé por qué tu risa
tiene ese són de maraca
y esa escalera graciosa
de canto de paraulata.

    Si te escondieras de noche
se asustaría la neblina
porque eres, negra, tan negra,
que tu pizarrón de carne
la noche se vuelve tiza.

    Si te escondieras de noche
nadie te podría encontrar.
Pero te ríes... y tu risa
es tan de ti y nadie más,
que el corazón te adivina
con suma facilidad.

    Después del cabestro el potro
y antes que el potro el bozal.
¡El corazón te adivina
con suma facilidad!

YOUR SMILE

Manuel Rodríguez-Cárdenas

An ear of corn would envy
your teeth of hulled maize
when you laugh at the pleasures
my hand gives you, black girl.

I don't know why your laughter
has that sound of the maraca
and that delightful range
of the song of the thrush.

If you hid yourself at night,
you would frighten the fog
because you are black, so black,
that on your slate-colored skin
night becomes chalk.

If you hid yourself at night
no one would find you.
But then you'd laugh... your own
special laugh
and my heart would find you
with the greatest ease.

Behind the halter the colt
in front of the colt the harness.
My heart would find you
with the greatest ease!

LA CANCIÓN DE LA NEGRITA

Manuel Rodríguez-Cárdenas

¡Consuelo Ruiz! ¡Consuelo Ruiz!
¿Qué has hecho, Consuelo Ruiz?
Has roto la maromera
gracia del Ton Toronjil,
con tu falda sandunguera
y ese andar de la cadera
que se sube a la nariz.

Deja a la niña altanera
que juegue sobre el tapiz.
Tu risa taratatera,
tus dientes de ajonjolí
y esa mano forastera
no sirven, Consuelo Ruiz,
para pisar la escalera
tenue del Ton Toronjil.

Tú eres negra jabequera,
caliente como el anís;
eres parche, río, bandera,
grito de sol somalí,
rica nave costanera
que naufragó en la frontera
frente al Cabo Guardafui.

Eres copla mañanera,
pescado para freír,
salto de boa, sonajera,
tambor que ruge feliz,
trote de la hembra cerrera
detrás del macho cerril.
Pero, ¡por Dios!, la escalera
tenue del Ton Toronjil,
no se hizo para ti.
¡Ni para mí!

THE SONG OF THE "NEGRITA"

Manuel Rodríguez-Cárdenas

    Consuelo Ruiz! Consuelo Ruiz!
What have you done, Consuelo Ruiz?
You have broken the acrobatic
grace of Ton Toronjil,
with your swishing skirt
and that hip-swaying walk
that makes the heart flutter.

    Let the arrogant child
play on the rug.
Your high-brow laughter,
your teeth of sesame
and your exotic hand,
will not help you, Consuelo Ruiz,
to walk up the fancy
staircase of Ton Toronjil.

    You are an unpolished black girl,
as hot as anise;
you are drum, river, flag,
shout of the Somalian sun,
rich coastal ship
which shipwrecked on the shore
near Cabo Guardafui.

    You are a morning song,
fish for frying,
a boa's leap, a baby's rattle,
a drum beating happily,
walk of an untamed woman
behind a wild man.
But, Lord, the fancy staircase
of Ton Toronjil,
was not made for you.
Nor for me!

Miguel Otero Silva

Venezuelan novelist, essayist, and poet Miguel Otero Silva was born in 1908. His poetic works include *Agua y cauce* (River and River Bed), 1937; *25 poemas*, 1942; *Elegía coral a Andrés Eloy Blanco* (Coral Elegy to Andrés Eloy Blanco), 1958; and *Umbral* (Threshold), 1966. He is the author of four novels: *Fiebre* (Fever), 1940; *Casas muertas* (Dead Houses), 1955; *Oficina No. 1* (Office Number 1), 1964; and *La muerte de Honorio* (The Death of Honorio), 1963. Some of his novels have appeared in German, Russian, French, and Italian translations.

Otero's novels and poetry reveal a profound preoccupation with the pain and suffering experienced by mankind. He expresses a genuine affinity of feeling and kinship with men, irrespective of race. In his poem "Yo no conozco a Cuba" (I Have Never Been to Cuba) from the collection *Agua y cauce*, he empathizes with the plight of the Afro-Cubans whom he refers to as "brothers":

> Mi corazón repica el ritmo negro
> que esparcen en la noche
> la clave y el bongó.
>
> My heart beats with the black rhythm
> scattered in the night
> by the *clave* and the bongo.

In another poem from this volume, "Negro Lorenzo", Otero expresses, from a black perspective, an understanding of the hardships and anguish which are inherent in the black experience in Latin America:

> Yo soy el Negro Lorenzo,
> nieto y bisnieto de esclavos,
> cruzado de cicatrices
> como negro tronco de árbol.
>
> I am the black Lorenzo,
> grandson and great grandson of slaves,
> slashed with scars
> like a black tree trunk.

But Lorenzo is not portrayed as a docile black, so often depicted in Latin American literature; rather he is a strong and rebellious man who refuses to be a slave:

> Los negros muertos esclavos,
> mi abuelo y mi bisabuelo.
> Negra y rebelde es mi mano.
>
> The dead black slaves,
> my grandfather and great-grandfather.
> My hand is black and rebellious.

In his poem "La infancia" (Childhood), from his book *Umbral*, Otero Silva evokes childhood experiences and impressions, the most vivid of which relate to an association with the *Negra* Marcolina, whom the poet credits with more wisdom than his conventionally educated father. As a repository of natural wisdom who often functions as mediator between Man and the supernatural world, Marcolina represents an important motif in Latin American literature.

LA INFANCIA

Miguel Otero Silva

Yo tenía siete años y un perro. Entonces
amaba la altanera retórica del mar.
Recuerdo las catorce casas de palma,
la escuela y su coral abecedario,
la capilla con su cruz a cuestas
y el calabozo de bahareque. ¿Por qué
el comisario encerraba entre murciélagos
los sábados
al único borracho, Antonio Sánchez,
o tal vez Antonio Salazar?

Al empañarse la tarde me alejaba del caserío
guiado por las huellas de las cabras o por la sombra
caminante de los alcatraces hasta los cardones.
El cardonal
manteníase en armas, comandante del viento
y de las mariposas amarillas.

Un domingo de octubre (yo no la había invitado)
me acompañó una muchacha del vecindario.
Era seiscientas noches mayor que yo
y le maduraban dos gemidos de amor en el pecho.
Cuando llegamos a las dunas donde se pone el sol
se tendió a mi lado, pez náufrago en la arena
comenzó a besarme con una boca
de aguamala herida. Sentí un miedo quemador y dulce:
no sabía si romper a llorar
o si esponja, musgo, raíz, trenzarme a su blancura.

Yo creía en San Miguel,
en los fantasmas,
en las brujas.

CHILDHOOD

Miguel Otero Silva

I was seven years old and had a dog. Then
I loved the arrogant rhetoric of the sea.
I remember the fourteen palm huts,
the school with its coral primer,
the chapel with its cross on the back
and the jailhouse with its mud walls. Why
did the sheriff lock up among the bats
on Saturdays
the only town drunk, Antonio Sánchez,
or was his name Antonio Salazar?

Late in the afternoons I left the village
guided by goat tracks or by the shadow
moving from the pelicans to the cacti.
The cactus field
kept itself armed, commander of the wind
and the yellow butterflies.

One October Sunday (I did not invite her)
a girl from the neighborhood went with me.
She was six hundred nights older than I
and two sparks of love were growing on her chest.
When we got to the dunes where the sun sets
she lay at my side, shipwrecked fish on the sand,
and began to kiss me with a mouth
of a wounded jellyfish. Feeling a sweet, burning fear,
I did not know whether to cry
or attach myself, like a sponge, moss or root to her whiteness.

I still believed in St. Michael,
in ghosts,
in witches.

Como no iba a creer si la negra Marcolina
me los había mostrado con su largo dedo de bejuco
encaramados a las rocas en tanto el crepúsculo humedecía
en espumas sus frentes pensativas. Y luego
ya no estaban ahí sino entre las jarcias de la madrugada,
vuela que vuela en círculos salobres sobre mi pequeño
y asustado corazón.

La negra Marcolina era cambiante y agorera como el mar.
Había días tranquilos en que caminaba por la playa
soledosa, llorando a su negrito muerto,
y otros atardeceres encrespados en que salía de la capilla,
de la penumbra acorralada donde conversaba con las ánimas benditas,
para anunciar a gritos el fin del mundo.

El cataclismo estuvo a punto de suceder cinco años antes
cuando el cometa Halley pasó muy cerca de nosotros
y se perdió en los barrancos lívidos del aire.
Sin embargo,
Marcolina predicaba que el pavo real de fuego
volvería enfurecido de sus infiernos
a trocar nuestros huesos en ceniza y lágrimas
"tal como destruyó Jehovah a Sodoma, a Gomorra
y a las ciudades vecinas."

Mi padre era todavía un tendero pobre
(vendía sombreros y anzuelos a los pescadores)
pero mi padre había leído a Renan y a Flammarion.
Ninguno sino él los había leído
en muchas leguas a la redonda.

Le preguntaban si era cierto que se acababa el mundo.

Sonreía muy seguro de sus libros
y contestaba:
La tierra será esta misma tierra
y el hombre será este mismo hombre
dentro de millones y millones de años.

Entonces Marcolina se echaba a reír.

How could I not believe when the black Marcolina
had shown them to me with her long rattan finger,
climbing the rocks while the twilight dampened
their pensive brows with foam. And suddenly
they were not there but among the trappings of morning,
flying in white circles above my small
and frightened heart.

The black Marcolina was moody and clairvoyant, like the sea.
There were calm days when she walked along the beach,
lonely, mourning her dead black boy,
on other breezy afternoons when she left the small chapel,
that silent place where she spoke to the blessed spirits,
to announce, in a loud voice, the end of the world.

The catastrophe almost occurred five years before
when Halley's Comet passed so close to us
and got lost in the livid hollows of the atmosphere.
Nevertheless,
Marcolina predicted that the flaming peacock
would return infuriated from its infernos
to change our bones to ashes and tears
"the same way Jehovah destroyed Sodom,
Gomorra and neighboring cities."

My father was still a poor shopkeeper
(selling hats and fishhooks to the fishermen)
but my father had read Renan and Flammarion.
The only one for miles around
who had read them.

People asked him if the world was really coming to an end.

He would smile, confident in his books
and answer:
The earth will be the same earth
and man will be the same man
millions and millions of years from now.

Then Marcolina would begin to laugh.

Notes

1 Sambrano Urdaneta and Miliani, *Literatura hispanoamericana*, II (Caracas: Editorial Texto, 1971), p. 199. "He abandonado la vida de poeta. No quiere esto decir que ya no escriba versos. Siempre los escribo; los escribo continuamente; pero siempre en las horas que me deja libre la política. No vivo en diferenciación; y no ha sido voluntad mía. Entré a la lucha política, muy jóven; y la realidad me obligó. A veces quisiera volver plenamente a la literatura; pero si me decidiera a hacerlo, quizá no podría; no es que me llamen las multitudes en calidad de líder político; es que mientras haya cien hombres y cien mujeres que me pidan no abandonar un campo en el que mi palabra podría ser beneficiosa, yo no tendría el derecho de desoírlos. La política, pues, obliga como un arte."
2 Sambrano Urdaneta and Miliani, II, p. 206. "Más que un político, soy un hombre de letras; un poeta prestado por la poesía a la política, en nombre de la responsabilidad del pensamiento. Si algo puedo representar en la lucha es la insurgencia contra el aislamiento olímpico del cultivador de belleza, el aislamiento en la asignatura de la preocupación social, el contacto con la tierra y los seres; la conciencia del deber humano que tiene faenas constructivas para toda la fila que corre del juglar al albañil . . ."
3 Ruiz del Vizo, *Poesía negra*, p. 157. "Andrés Eloy Blanco fue y es el más popular de los poetas venezolanos, fama que le vino no sólo por su destacada actuación en la vida pública de la nación, no sólo por su altísima obra de poeta, sino por haber captado el alma popular, las tradiciones venezolanas como nadie."
4 Mónica Mansour, *La poesía negrista* (Mexico: Ediciones Era, 1973), pp. 119-20. "Su poema 'Píntame angelitos negros', a la vez ingenuo y lleno de amargura, expresa la injusticia que han sufrido los negros en Venezuela y en América. La amargura llega hasta la idea de un cielo hecho por los blancos, donde también existe la injusticia."
5 Rosa E. Valdés-Cruz, *La poesía negroide en América* (New York: Las Américas, 1970), p. 170. "Nace Rodríguez-Cárdenas en el estado de Yaracay en 1912 y se siente fuertemente impresionado por el folklore de la población negra de este estado."
6 Stanley A. Cyrus, "The Development of Black Literature in

Hispanic America", lecture.
[7] Julián Padrón, "Presentación de Manuel Rodríguez-Cárdenas", in Manuel Rodríguez-Cárdenas, *Tambor* (Caracas: 1938), n. pag. "La autobiografía, como en todo libro inicial, ronda por estos poemas con un regusto de sensaciones vividas, de las cuales surge cernida brava poesía."
[8] Eusebia Cosme, well-known reciter of Afro-Hispanic poetry.
[9] *Dale, dale*, an expression of encouragement and support for the dancer. It is similar to the asides that are a part of the flamenco dance tradition, with the aim of making the dancers more animated.

Works Cited

Alín, José María. *El cancionero español de tipo tradicional.* Madrid: Taurus, 1968.

Anderson Imbert, Enrique. *Historia de la literatura hispanoamericana.* Mexico: Fondo de Cultura Económica, 5th ed., 1966.

Arrom, José Juan. "Presencia del negro en la poesía folklórica americana," in *Certidumbre de America.* Havana, 1959; rpt. Madrid: Gredos, 1971.

Artel, Jorge. *Tambores en la noche.* Cartagena, Colombia: Editora Bolívar, 1940.

Boulware, Kay. "Woman and Nature in *Negrismo.*" *Studies in Afro-Hispanic Literature.* I (1977), 16-25.

Brindis de Salas, Virginia. *Pregón de Marimorena.* Montvideo: Sociedad Cultural Editora Indoamericana, 1946.

Brooks, John. "Slavery and the Slave in the Works of Lope de Vega." *Romanic Review*, 19 (1928), 232-43.

Cartey, Wilfred. *Black Images.* New York: Teachers College Press, 1970.

Castellano, Juan. "El negro esclavo en el entremés del Siglo de Oro." *Hispania*, 44 (1961), 55-65.

Chasca, Edmund de. "The Phonology of the Speech of Negroes in Early Spanish Drama." *Hispanic Review*, 14 (1946), 322-39.

Cobb, Martha. "Afro-Arabs, Blackamoors and Blacks: An Inquiry into Race Concepts Through Spanish Literature." *Black World*, 21, No.4 (1972), 32-40.

Coulthard, G.R. *Race and Colour in Caribbean Literature.* London: Oxford University Press, 1962.

Cyrus, Stanley A. *El cuento negrista sudamericano.* Quito: Editorial Casa de la Cultura Ecuatoriana, 1973.

_____. "The Development of Black Literature in Hispanic America." NEH Workshop, Hampton Institute, Virginia. 3 June 1978.

De Costa, Miriam. "The Evolution of the 'Tema Negro' in Literature of the Spanish Baroque." *CLA Journal*, 17 (1974), 417-30.

_____. "The Portrayal of Blacks in a Spanish Medieval Manuscript." *Negro History Bulletin*, 37 (1974), 192-96.

García-Barrio, Constance Sparrow de. "The Image of the Black Man in the

Poetry of Nicolás Guillén." In *Blacks in Hispanic Literature.* Ed. Miriam De Costa. Port Washington, N.Y.: Kennikat Press, 1977, pp. 105-13.

Jackson, Richard L. *Black Writers in Latin America.* Albuquerque: University of New Mexico Press, 1979.

──────. *The Black Image in Latin American Literature.* Albuquerque: University of New Mexico Press, 1976.

Johnson, Lemuel A. *The Devil, the Gargoyle, and the Buffoon: The Negro as Metaphor in Western Literature.* Port Washington, N.Y.: Kennikat Press, 1969, 1971.

Mansour, Mónica. *La poesía negrista.* Mexico: Ediciones Era, 1973.

Martán Góngora, Helcías. *Suma poética (1963-1968).* Bogotá: Biblioteca del Instituto Colombiano de Cultura Hispánica, Ediciones de la Revista Ximenez de Quesada, 1969.

Meléndez, Concha. *Signos de Iberoamérica.* Mexico: Imp. Manuel León Sánchez, 1936. "Sor Juana y los negros," pp. 83-88.

Monguío, Luis. "El negro en algunos poetas españoles y americanos anteriores a 1800." *Revista Iberoamericana,* 22 (1957), 245-59.

Morales, Jorge Luis. *Poesía afroantillana y negrista: Puerto Rico, República Domicana, Cuba.* Río Piedras: Editorial Universitaria, 1976.

Noble, Enrique. *Literatura afro-hispanoamericana.* Lexington, Massachusetts: Xerox College Publishing, 1973.

Onís, Federico de. Introduction to Luis Palés Matos, *Poesía.* San Juan: Editorial Universidad de Puerto Rico, 1957.

Ortiz, Adalberto. *El animal herido.* Quito: Editorial Casa de la Cultura Ecuatoriana, 1970.

──────. "Negritude in Latin American Culture." In *Blacks in Hispanic Literature.* Ed. Miriam De Costa. Port Washington, N.Y.: Kennikat Press, 1977, pp. 74-82.

Ortiz, Fernando and Rafael Marquina. "The Negro in the Spanish Theatre." *Phylon,* 4 (1943), 147-52. Translation by E. Irene Diggs.

Otero Silva, Miguel. *Poesía completa.* Caracas: Monte Avila Editores, 1972.

Padrón, Julio. "Presentación de Manuel Rodríguez-Cárdenas." In Manuel Rodríguez-Cárdenas. *Tambor.* Caracas, 1938. N. pag.

Palés Matos, Luis. *Poesía (1915-1956).* San Juan: Editorial Universidad de Puerto Rico, 1957.

Quevedo, Francisco. *Obras Completas,* Vol. I. Barcelona: Editorial Planeta, 1971.

Rodríguez-Cárdenas, Miguel. *Tambor: Poemas para negros y mulatos.* Caracas: Editorial "Elite", 1938.

Rout, Leslie B. Jr. *The African Experience in Latin America: 1502 to the*

Present Day. London: Cambridge University Press, 1976.

Ruiz del Vizo, Hortensia. *Black Poetry of the Americas: A Bilingual Anthology*. Miami: Ediciones Universal, 1972.

———. *Poesia negra del Caribe y otras áreas*. Miami: Ediciones Universal, 1972.

Rushing, Andrea B. "Images of Black Women in Modern African Poetry." In *Sturdy Black Bridges: Visions of Black Women in Literature*. Ed. Roseann Bell, Bettye J. Parker, and Beverly Guy-Sheftall. New York: Doubleday, 1979, pp. 18-24.

Salas, Teresa C. and Henry J. Richards. "Nicomedes Santa Cruz y la poesía de su conciencia de negritud." *Cuadernos Americanos*, No. 202 (1975), pp. 182-99.

Sambrano Urdaneta, Oscar and Domingo Miliani. *Literatura hispano-americana: Manual/Antologia*, Vol. I. Caracas: Editorial Texto, 1971.

Sampson, Margaret. "Africa in Medieval Spanish Literature: Its Appearance in *El Caballero Cifar*." *Negro History Bulletin* 32 (1969), 14-18.

Santa Cruz, Nicomedes. *Ritmos negros del Perú*. Buenos Aires: Editorial Losada, S.A., 1971.

Sayers, Raymond S. "The Negro in the Literature of the Iberian Peninsula." In his *The Negro in Brazilian Literature*. New York: Hispanic Institute in the United States, 1956.

Spratlin, Velaurez B. "The Negro in Spanish Literature." In *Blacks in Hispanic Literature*. Ed. Miriam De Costa. Port Washington, N.Y.: Kennikat Press, 1977, pp. 47-52.

Valdés-Cruz, Rosa E. *La poesía negriodè en América."* New York: Las Américas, 1970.

Wardropper, Bruce. "The Color Problem in Spanish Traditional Poetry." *MLN*, 75 (1960), pp. 415-20.

Woodson, Carter G. "Attitudes of the Iberian Peninsula (In Literature)." In *Blacks in Hispanic Literature*. Ed. Miriam De Costa. Port Washington, N.Y.: Kennikat Press, 1977, pp. 36-46.

Wynter, Sylvia. "The Eye of the Other: Images of the Black in Spanish Literature." In *Blacks in Hispanic Literature*. Ed. Miriam De Costa. Port Washington, N.Y.: Kennikat Press, 1977, pp. 8-19.

Young, Ann Venture. "The Black Woman in Afro-Caribbean Poetry." In *Blacks in Hispanic Literature*. Ed. Miriam De Costa. Port Washington, N.Y.: Kennikat Press, 1977, pp. 137-42.

Works Consulted

Allen, Alma. "Literary Relations Between Spain and Africa." *Journal of Negro History*, 50 (1965), 97-105.
Arroyo, Anita. *America en su literatura*. San Juan: Ediciones de la Torre, Universidad de Puerto Rico, 1967.
Ballagas, Emilio. *Mapa de la poesia negra*. Buenos Aires: Editorial Pleamar, 1946; rpt. Lichtenstein: Kraus, 1970.
Becco, H.J. *El tema del negro en bailes, cantos y villancicos de los siglos XVI y XVII*. Buenos Aires: Ollantay, 1951.
Manrique Cabrera, Francisco. *Historia de la literatura puertorriqueña*. Río Piedras: Editorial Cultural, 1971.
Cobb, Martha K. "Africa in Latin America: Customs, Culture, Literature." *Black World* 21, No. 10 (1972), 4-19.
_____. "A Bibliographical Essay: An Appraisal of Latin American Slavery Through Literature." *Journal of Negro History*, 58 (1973), 460-69.
_____. "Concepts of Blackness in the Poetry of Nicolás Guillén, Jacques Roumain and Langston Hughes." *CLA Journal*, 18 (1974), 262-72.
Coleman, Ben C. "Black Themes in the Literature of the Caribbean." *The Rican: A Journal of Contemporary Puerto Rican Thought*. No. 3 (Spring 1973), pp. 48-54.
De Costa, Miriam. "Nicolás Guillén and his Poetry for Afro-Americans." *Black World*, 22, No. 11 (1973), 12-16.
Diggs, Irene. "Color in Colonial Spanish America." *Journal of Negro History*, 38 (1953), 403-27.
_____. "The Negro in the Viceroyalty of Rio de la Plata." *Journal of Negro History*, 36 (1951), 281-90.
Ebersole, A.V. "Black is Beautiful in Seventeenth Century Spain." *Romance Notes*, 12 (1971), 387-91.
Estupiñán Bass, Nelson. *Canto negro por la luz: poemas para negros y blancos*. Esmeraldas, Ecuador: Ediciones del Núcleo Privincial de Esmeraldas de la Casa de la Cultura Ecuatoriana, 1954.
Fernández de la Vega, Oscar and Alberto N. Pamies. *Iniciación a la poesía afro-americana*. Miami: Ediciones Universal, 1973.
Franco, Jean. *The Modern Culture of Latin America: Society and the*

Artist. Middlesex, England: Penguin Books Ltd., 1970.
Freyre, Gilberto. *The Masters and the Slaves.* New York: Alfred A. Knopf, 1946.
Gómez-Gil, Orlando. "La poesía popular: poesía negra o afroantillana." In his *Historia crítica de la literatura hispanoamericana: desde los orígenes hasta el momento actual.* New York: Holt, Rinehart and Winston, 1968, pp. 650-52.
Guillén, Nicolás. *Sóngoro Cosongo: poemas mulatos.* Havana: Ucar García, 1931.
Guirao, Ramón. *Orbita de la poesía afrocubana.* Havana: 1938.
Herring, Hubert. "The African Background." In his *A History of Latin America.* New York: Alfred A. Knopf, 1962, pp. 93-116.
Jackson, Richard L. "'Mestizaje' vs. Black Identity: The Color Crisis in Latin America." *Black World,* 24, No. 9 (1975), 4-21.
_____. "Some Recent Studies on Blacks in Hispanic Literature." *American Hispanist,* 15, No. 2 (1977), 2-3.
Jason, Howard M. "The Negro in Spanish Literature to the End of the 'Siglo de Oro'." *CLA Journal,* 9 (1965), 121-31.
Lapesa, Rafael. *Historia de la lengua española.* Madrid: Escelier, S.L., 1955.
Knight, Franklin W. *Slave Society in Cuba During the Nineteenth Century.* Madison: University of Wisconsin Press, 1970.
_____. *The African Dimension in Latin American Societies.* New York: Macmillan, 1974.
Martán Góngora, Helcías. *Suma poética: 1963-1968.* Bogotá: Biblioteca del Instituto Colombiano de Cultura Hispánica, 1969.
Martín, José Luis. "Lírica postnerudiana: poesía negroide." In *Literatura hispanoamericana contemporánea.* Río Piedras: Editorial Edil, 1973, pp. 82-97
Matheus, John F. "African Footprints in Hispanic American Literature." *Journal of Negro History,* 23 (1938), 265-89.
Olivera, Otto. "La mujer de color en la poesía de Nicolás Guillén." In *Homenaje a Lydia Cabrera.* Reinaldo Sánchez, et al. Miami: Ediciones Universal, 1978, pp. 165-74.
Olliz Boyd, Antonio. "The Concept of Black Awareness as a Thematic Approach in Latin American Literature." In *Blacks in Hispanic Literature.* Ed. Miriam De Costa. Port Washington, N.Y.: Kennikat Press, 1977, pp. 65-73
Ortiz, Adalberto. *El animal herido.* Quito: Editorial Casa de la Cultura Ecuatoriana, 1959; rpt. Lichtenstein: Kraus, 1970.
_____. *Tierra, son y tambor: Cantares negros y mulatos.* Mexico: Ed. La Cigarra, 1945.
Pereda Valdés, Ildefonso. *Antología de la poesía negra americana.*

Santiago de Chile, 1936; rpt. Buenos Aires: Editorial Pleamar, 1946.

Pescatello, Ann M. *The African in Latin America.* New York: Alfred Knopf, 1975.

_____. *Female and Male in Latin America.* University of Pittsburgh, 1973.

Rama, Carlos M. "The Passing of the Afro-Uruguayans from Caste Society to Class Society." In *Race and Class in Latin America.* Ed. Magnus Morner. New York: Columbia University Press, 1970.

Rushing, Andrea Benton. "Annotated Bibliography of Black Women in Black Literature." *CLA Journal,* 21 (1978), 435-42.

_____. "The Changing Same: Black Women in Afro-American Poetry." *Black World,* 24, No. 11 (1975), 18-30.

Salazar Valdés, Hugo. *Carbones en el alba.* Bogotá: Editorial Iqueima, 1951.

_____. *Las raices sonoras.* Cali, 1976.

Sims, Edna N. "Notes on the Negative Image of Woman in Spanish Literature." *CLA Journal* 19 (1976), 468-83.

Tannenbaum, Frank. *Slave and Citizen: The Negro in the Americas.* New York: Alfred A. Knopf, 1946.

Weber de Kurlat, F. "Sobre el negro como tipo cómico en el teatro español del siglo XVI." *Romance Philology,* 17 (1963), 380-91.

West, Robert C. *The Pacific Lowlands of Colombia.* Baton Rouge: Louisiana State University Press, 1957.

Whitten, Norman E. Jr. *Black Frontiersman: A South American Case.* Cambridge, Massachusetts: Schenkman Publishing Company, 1974.

Wilson, Leslie N. "El negro en la poesía hispanoamericana." *CLA Journal,* 13 (1970), 335-49.

Zelinsky, W. "The Historical Geography of the Negro Population of Latin America." *Journal of American History,* 34 (1949), 153-221.

OHIO UNIVERS